PROTECT YOURSELF
at College

PROTECT YOURSELF

at *College*

Smart Choices—Safe Results

THOMAS M. KANE

CAPITAL
BOOKS, INC.
Sterling, Virginia

Copyright © 2008 Thomas M. Kane

Capital Books, Inc.
P.O. Box 605
Herndon, Virginia 20172-0605

ISBN 978-1-933102-61-0

Library of Congress Cataloging-in-Publication Data

Kane, Thomas M.
Protect yourself at college : smart choices—safe results / Thomas M. Kane.
p. cm.
ISBN 978-1-933102-61-0
1. College students—Crimes against—United States—Prevention. 2. Universities and colleges—Security measures—United States. I. Title.

HV6250.4.S78K36 2008
613.60835'0973—dc22

2007050321

Printed in the United States of America on acid-free paper that meets the American National Standards Institute Z39-48 Standard.

First Edition

10 9 8 7 6 5 4 3 2

This book is dedicated to anyone who has lost a loved one or friend while attending college.

It is my sincere hope that the information provided in this book will somehow prevent such personal tragedies from ever happening again.

CONTENTS

FOREWORD

Being a police officer can be a difficult and dangerous job. It is an unpredictable profession where stress creeps in on numerous levels. Unfortunately, it can be deadly. Yet, there are days when the rewards are many. The fulfillment and gratification officers feel knowing that they have made a difference in someone's life are why they come to work each day.

Regardless of the size city or town, every community throughout the country has its own challenges and problems. However, when a college or major university is located in your jurisdiction, those challenges can be magnified when dealing with potentially tens of thousands of young adult students and visitors.

Ask police officers, rookies or veterans, about the most difficult incident or troubling times on the job, and more often than not they will tell you it is when teens or young adults are involved. It is heartbreaking when a young person is the victim of a senseless crime or an accident that results in serious injury or death. I know firsthand. I am Chief Tom King, Chief of Police of State College, Pennsylvania, home of the Pennsylvania State University.

State College is a relatively rural town in central Pennsylvania. It's a wonderfully diverse community whose residents have a sense of pride in calling State College their home. Many refer to our community as Happy Valley. Our police department employs sixty-five police officers serving the town and two surrounding communities. I have been privileged to be a State College Police Officer for more than twenty-six years, the past fifteen as Chief of Police.

Penn State University has a separate police department with approximately fifty police officers on the University Park campus. They are an outstanding police department whose officers have fully sworn capabilities. Our police department is very fortunate to have a great working relationship with them. In addition to working many events together, our departments serve as each other's primary backup for day-to-day calls.

So, what makes for a safe community? What makes for a safe college campus? As a student, are your security expectations realistic regarding the level of protection law enforcement is able to provide? As a parent, have you equipped your children heading off to college with the necessary tools to keep them as safe as possible?

Students become victims for many reasons. For the first time in their lives, students enter into the independent world of college life. They are on their own after eighteen years of close supervision. Now they're at an age when they begin to take more risks. They tend not to think or be concerned about the inherent dangers. They begin to experiment more. They feel invincible.

When alcohol is added to the equation, and students engage in activities they have not experienced, the propensity for injury increases dramatically. A lack of knowledge and concern about their vulnerabilities is often why young people become victims or are involved in accidents. This is not to say students are always careless or reckless. It simply means they do not have enough life experiences to regularly make proper safety decisions. Because they fear little, they inadvertently put themselves in potentially dangerous situations.

One area that puts many students at significant risk is excessive drinking. While those who engage in dangerous drinking are at greatest risk, even those who do not drink or who drink "responsibly" are often at risk from the secondary effects of dangerous drinking. When students drink excessively, crimes and accidents occur. Some pass out in yards, urinate in public, start fights, damage vehicles, steal property, commit sexual assaults, and engage in other criminal activity. Students who drink to excess will most likely end up with legal, medical, social, and academic problems.

Parents who send their children to college ask me regularly, "Is the drinking really any different today than it was thirty years ago?" I tell them, "Yes, it is different on two fronts." First, intoxication levels are higher than they were several decades ago. Second, there's an increase in the frequency in which students engage in high-level or dangerous drinking. Many students report they engage in high-risk or dangerous drinking eight to ten times a month.

Another area that has had an impact is the use of technology. MySpace, Facebook, YouTube, and text messaging did not exist ten years ago, much less thirty years ago. Thousands of students can be mobilized and pour into the streets almost instantly with text messaging. Sometimes, the videos or photos posted on such sites show illegal activity that leads to a criminal investigation by the police department. Two other serious and rapidly growing crimes that place students and other adults at risk are identity theft and Internet fraud.

The victimization of young people must be reduced. Parents need to educate their teens about potential dangers during the middle and high school years so students can start guarding their safety prior to arriving at college. Parents have countless opportunities to inform or educate their child about college safety during the teen years as situations arise. These "teaching moments" provide parents excellent opportunities to discuss actual incidents with their teen. Real, factual incidents that *do* occur versus those harms that *may* occur tend to resonate with all of us, and especially with young people.

Although close parental supervision is absent once a student arrives on campus, parents still play an influential role. Research has shown that when parents discuss dangerous drinking and other safety issues with their child, they can lower the risk of their student engaging in high-risk activities.

Colleges and universities must continue to find strategies to reduce student victimization and high-risk activities. This can be done through education and programming. Parents should be alert to the types of programs and services colleges and universities have to prevent or combat situations that place students at risk. For example, what type of student orientation does the institution provide? There is so much for a first-year student to learn about the school, about the community, and about living independently.

I speak to students on a regular basis, and they want more general "life skills" information. Most colleges and universities have brief, single-day orientations. I believe strongly that students would be served better if colleges and universities adopted an orientation curriculum taught weekly over the entire first semester. This would allow students to be taught about their social and civic responsibilities on and off campus, about the dangers specific to their new community and school, about the various high-risk situations they could face, about the nuances and laws of the community, about what services are available to them, and other important topics. Freshmen need such information, but they don't always get it.

Many college students across the country do become victims either by their own doing or at the hands of others. Some of the unfortunate incidents have resulted in serious injury or even death. Needless to say, families have been shattered. Unfortunately, in my twenty-seven years of law enforcement, I have seen most everything.

The author of this book, Thomas M. Kane, has spent many years investigating and studying the crimes and accidents that occur on or around college campuses—his work provides important safety information for students to better prepare them for their college career.

Protect Yourself at College is a comprehensive resource highlighting those areas that put students at risk. The stories and precautions suggested throughout this book can aid in reducing the risk of a student becoming a victim of a crime or an accident. With a little effort, young people everywhere can have a safer college experience and avoid becoming a statistic.

CHIEF THOMAS R. KING
STATE COLLEGE POLICE DEPARTMENT
STATE COLLEGE, PENNSYLVANIA

ACKNOWLEDGMENTS

The challenges of writing a book and the time it takes are enormous. To say that I am grateful to my wife, Lee Ann, and daughter, Lindsay, for their patience and assistance while writing this book would be an understatement. They are both truly a gift in my life!

To my family, especially my mother and father, Barbara and Richard Kane, thank you for all that you do. I love you both!

A special thank you to Dan O'Keefe, a wonderful friend who took an incredible amount of time to edit the entire manuscript. There is no way this book would have been completed on time if it were not for Dano.

I'd like to thank Chief Thomas R. King, Chief of Police of State College, Pennsylvania, for taking time from his busy schedule to write the foreword.

I want to acknowledge the folks who have shared their stories so that others may learn from their misfortunes. I am especially thankful to Debbie and Greg Smith, who allowed me to be a part of something so personal.

In alphabetical order, I am extremely grateful to Mr. Mike Halligan, president of the Center for Campus Fire Safety and associate director of Environmental Health and Safety at the University of Utah; Dr. Ralph W. Hingson, ScD, MPH, director of the Division of Epidemiology and Prevention Research at the National Institute of Alcohol Abuse and Alcoholism; Professor Hank Nuwer, author of the book *Wrongs of Passage*; Monsignor Robert Sheeran, president of Seton Hall University; Dr. Jason Winkle, PhD, president of the International Tactical Officers Training Association; and Dr. Donald W. Zeigler, PhD, of the American Medical Association.

Thanks to my friends, Keith and Amy Brown, Joe Sabo, Matt and Linda Valentine, and Joe Zuravleff, your friendship, continued support, and encouragement are appreciated more than I can express.

Finally, I am very appreciative to Amy Fries, senior editor at Capital Books, and Kathleen Hughes, publisher, who both recognize the importance of bringing the first comprehensive college safety book ever written to the marketplace.

INTRODUCTION

Years before the Virginia Tech shooting of April 2007, I began to notice an increase in the number of crimes and accidents on America's college campuses.

I'm a news junkie. It seemed as though every time I opened the newspaper, logged on to the Internet, or watched the evening news, there was a story of a college student who was killed, seriously injured, or the victim of a crime. Was the media covering these incidents with greater frequency? Was I simply becoming more aware? Were America's college campuses under a recent siege of criminal activity? I was unsure, but the news reports were disturbing.

There were stories of students being hurt in car accidents, falling out of dorm windows, and drinking excessively. There were reports of females being raped in dorms, raped on campus, and raped on Spring Break. There were news accounts of students being severely injured in alcohol hazing incidents from a variety of groups, including fraternities and cheerleading squads. There appeared to be a rash of dorm fires, off-campus apartment fires, and everyday accidents. Week after week, I was left with the impression that there was a considerable increase in the number of crimes and accidents on college campuses.

I was wrong. After a brief examination of the statistics, I quickly learned that there was *not* an increase in the amount of crimes and accidents. As a matter of fact, a few crime categories actually experienced a reduction in the number of incidents reported. A reduction perhaps, but the numbers were still too high. With hundreds of thousands of college students either being victimized, arrested, or injured each year, the time had come to examine these excessively high numbers in greater detail.

I soon found many organizations already in place, which were involved, to varying degrees, in college safety issues. Some of these groups were formed by parents-turned-advocates after losing a child at college. Some groups were created by individuals who had some life-changing experience. Though they were all very specific in their purpose, I wanted to take a different approach.

I thought it would be prudent to identify where most of the crimes and accidents occurred. Where were students being victimized? What was the major cause of the incidents? I was curious if school administrators could have done more to prevent such occurrences. Could the parents do more? Were students just at the wrong place at the wrong time? Or were students acting like a bunch of knuckleheads and making poor choices that had life-altering results?

Depending on the source, a few of the numbers varied slightly; some were the same. A macabre curiosity came over me as I began to plow through the data. Each year 1,700 college students die from alcohol-related injuries. Another 1,200 students commit suicide. Tens of thousands of females are sexually assaulted. Over 100,000 students are arrested for liquor law violations, drug violations, arson, and weapons violations, just to name a few. There are burglaries, robberies, assaults, motor-vehicle thefts, and murders.

Critics will argue that given all the numbers above, college campuses are still incredibly safe. My response to that is, "Compared to what?" The numbers tell us that roughly 5 percent of all college students are victimized or hurt in one form or another. If your child is one of the hundreds of thousands of students who are victimized or injured, is that acceptable to you? I know of no other segment of society where a 5 percent victimization rate is acceptable.

The greater question is, are the numbers correct? The short answer is no! Under the Clery Act, which is examined in Chapter One, any college or university that receives federal funds must report its crime statistics and make them publicly available. The key word is "report." Many of the numbers are only what is being "reported." Colleges and universities are not required, for example, to report accidents. They are not required to report every incident that happens off campus. As history has shown, colleges and universities don't report every criminal act that happens on campus, either. Additionally, most sexual assaults go unreported. Incidents that occur on Spring Break are not included in any tally. Finally, if over 100,000 students are arrested each year for various violations, can you imagine the number of incidents that go undetected?

The bottom line is—the numbers are unacceptable. I cannot help but think of the collateral damage that is created every year. Families and friends are shattered. People have lost sons, daughters, and friends. Sexual assault victims are left with indelible scars. Affected students are left with academic, legal, and health problems. Innocent people are victimized and property is vandalized. Something had to be done.

In spring 2004, as I began my research, I had no idea if the information obtained would warrant the writing of a book. I knew that I couldn't walk into a bookstore and purchase a book on college safety. It just didn't exist. There were other books about various aspects of college life but nothing exclusively on protecting oneself at college.

It did not take years to draw a few conclusions regarding the state of safety on college campuses: colleges and universities are not doing enough to educate students about the potential hazards that exist on campuses. Parents tend to be rather naive regarding the dangers. Students have an air of invincibility that is exacerbated by their lack of experience in recognizing potentially dangerous situations. When you combine those factors and add excessive amounts of alcohol into the equation, it can create a set of circumstances so unique it's no wonder that the crime statistics are not three times what's actually reported. Or are they?

I have identified areas on campus and off campus where students have the greatest chance of becoming injured and victimized. I show how students put themselves in situations without realizing the potential dangers. I offer checklists of suggestions and safety precautions that will enable students to better protect themselves and their property.

Criminal activity and accidents on college campuses are a fact of life. No person or campus is exempt from that reality. The key to any safety situation is being proactive—knowing what can possibly happen in advance and knowing how to respond in the event something actually does happen.

For the Parents

This book is not designed to frighten you in any way. Its objective is not to make you worry every time you think about your child at college. In some way, I hope this book provides a reassuring level of comfort knowing that after your child has read it, he or she will be better prepared and better informed should an unforeseen incident arise.

I recognize the anxiety you may have as your child leaves for college. As the father of a teenager in high school, I share your concern. Although it's increasingly difficult to talk to teenagers and offer advice when they're away, stay involved. Try to use this book as a mechanism to bridge the gap in any communication challenges you may be experiencing.

Read this book yourself. Become familiar with the changes that have taken place since you went to school. Reacquaint yourself with those areas of campus life that have remained the same. If you're a parent who didn't attend college, your life experiences are nonetheless valuable and should be shared with your child.

As parents, we can't turn America's college campuses into fortresses—nor should we. Students need to experience the freedom and openness that college life offers. As parents, all we can do is continue to give them the tools we think they'll need in life to succeed and be happy. *Protect Yourself at College* is but one tool in that toolbox.

Throughout the book, you'll notice the "Hot Tip" sections, designed to emphasize a key point or suggestion. So you don't feel left out, here's one specifically for you.

✎ Hot Tip:
Buy your student a shredder as a high school graduation present.

For the Students

I think it would be a safe bet to say that the majority of you reading this book didn't purchase it. I understand that. More than likely, it was purchased by a parent or another relative and given to you as a gift. Although it was graciously accepted, some of you may have thought, "Great, in addition to my parents telling me what to do, now there's a book!" To ease any concerns you may have, let me tell you from the outset what this book will *not* do:

✓ It will *not* tell you: don't drink alcohol.

✓ It will *not* tell you: don't have sex.

✓ It will *not* tell you: don't try to sneak into the bars.

✓ It will *not* tell you: don't get home late at night.

✓ It will *not* tell you: don't go on Spring Break.

✓ It will *not* tell you: don't have your boyfriend or girlfriend sleep over.

✓ It will *not* tell you: don't be silly and embarrass yourself.

Did I leave anything out? If I did, you get the point. My intent is *not* to harp on you or become the moral police. The goal of this book is to bring awareness to the real dangers that exist on college campuses and offer suggestions to prevent you from becoming a crime or an accident statistic. Ideally, this book will teach you to recognize a dangerous situation *before* something unfortunate happens.

I don't discount the fact that you have exercised a great deal of responsibility and used caution when you were living at home. Most of you are probably dependable and conscientious young adults. Some of you may have experimented with alcohol. Chances are you're a reliable driver, one who doesn't drive recklessly. While your previous behavior is commendable, make no mistake, you will be living a different lifestyle once college begins. You can easily become victimized or end up in an unpleasant situation through no fault of your own.

No one expects to be in an accident. No one wakes up in the morning and says, "Hey, this is the day that I am going to be victimized on campus."

No matter what high-tech security features your college has in place, it's imperative that you take the lead role regarding your own safety. Own it! You must become proactive instead of reactive. You must train yourself to expect the unexpected. Don't set yourself up to become a target.

It's quite possible you believe your parents are overreacting or worrying too much by asking you to read this book. I assure you that they're not. The world is much different now than when your parents were in school. Please, try to cut your parents a break and understand their concern.

The stories throughout this book are true. The scenarios that are featured occur often. This book was written to provide you with the knowledge to make smart choices about your personal safety, choices that will produce safe results. It is my hope that this book makes your college experience more enjoyable. Have fun, but . . .

THOMAS M. KANE

PRESIDENT,

THE COLLEGE SAFETY ZONE

WWW.COLLEGESAFETYZONE.COM

1

Life in the Dorms

Ahhh, dorm life, it's great. There are no parents around and no brothers or sisters endlessly annoying you. More importantly, no curfews. You can eat what you want and dress how you like. Yes, you will have to share a bathroom with fifty other people, and more than likely, you'll be sharing your room with a stranger. But it's okay, because you're finally on your own. What better way to begin a book on college life and college safety than a chapter about your new home, the dorm.

Almost every incoming freshman begins the college years by staying in a campus dormitory. For most of you, attending college is the first time you've been away from home without some minimal supervision. Dorm living is great fun and will provide wonderful memories. Living in the dorms is an incredible learning experience that can foster lifelong relationships. Chances are your roommate, or someone you'll meet in the dorm, will become an everlasting friend, or possibly your spouse.

The built-in social life of dormitory living can have many upsides. There is an almost endless supply of willing people around if you need someone to help you study. If you're hanging out and want to grab a burger and soda, often someone on your floor will want to tag along. You'll go to the cafeteria with your roommate more times than you can imagine. Rainy and snowy weekends will be spent with other students from your dorm who don't feel like going anywhere.

Dorm living can also have its downside. With more than a hundred students living on your floor alone, it's difficult to escape the nonstop day-to-day interruptions. Friday and Saturday nights can become rather raucous, and patience can wear thin. Every now and then it's nice not to shower with twenty people. Sometimes you simply need a break from the communal lifestyle. When you're feeling the pressure from the lack of privacy, go visit a friend or take a road trip home to see your family and get a home-cooked meal. Before you have a chance to get homesick though, let's get you moved in first.

Move-In Day

I know, you're not even unpacked, and we're talking about security measures. Sorry about that, but someone has to tell you. Typically, move-in days are filled with confusion. Cars are lining the streets as far as you can see. People are buzzing in and out of the dorm carrying boxes and furniture. Parents are giving you their last little tidbits of advice. Upperclassmen are checking you in and assigning rooms, and the campus crook is sitting on the bench outside with a bottled water in hand, watching everything you are doing.

Move-in day is a criminal's paradise. They take inventory as thousands of students are piling into various dorms bringing all their newly purchased wares. They hang out in parking lots or peruse the sidewalk waiting for the optimum time to select their target. It's virtually impossible to distinguish who these people are, so exercise caution when unloading your car and carrying your belongings. Criminals know moving into your dorm can be overwhelming. With the confusion of the day, you can easily become distracted. Here are a few things to keep in mind for move-in day.

✓ Never leave your belongings unattended.
✓ Always lock your car when you're bringing in a load.
✓ Have a family member stay in your room while you unload more things.
✓ Bag or wrap a towel around valuables such as jewelry, laptops, or any other valuable possessions.
✓ If you must leave your room, make certain it is locked.

Roommates

More times than not, your roommate will be a complete stranger. You will bring your own set of habits and routines, and so will your new living partner. Having a roommate can present challenges, especially if you've never shared a room with anyone. There's no question it's an adjustment, but remain flexible. You may consider giving your new roommate the first choice of beds or closets. It could go a long way. Talk to your roommate and attempt to establish some ground rules. Discuss various chores, bedtime preferences, having visitors, music, and other concerns. Talk about sharing items like food, clothes, and computers. Setting up boundaries from the beginning is necessary for a successful roommate relationship.

Occasionally, a roommate will be completely incompatible with your lifestyle. It happens; don't worry about it. Just chalk it up to another life experience. If possible, don't give up right away; give it some time to work itself out. Depending on the severity of your differences, you may have to switch rooms. Attempt to do this with as little animosity and as much tact as possible. The first step is to notify your resident assistant (RA) or a campus housing official. If immediate room accommodations cannot be made until mid-semester, you may have to persevere until the end of the semester. Hang in there. It's only a short time. Try to turn this into a positive experience.

If you find that your roommate is into illegal activity, ask that your room be switched immediately. If your RA is unable to facilitate your request, head directly to administration. Do not think for one second that your roommate would not hide drugs in your belongings. Colleges reserve the right to inspect your room at anytime if they think there may be illegal activity going on. If drugs are found in your belongings, you may be expelled before you even have a chance of saying, "But they're not mine!"

Dorm life is somewhat like living in a fishbowl. You'll encounter not only students walking in and around the dorm, but also their guests. That doesn't make for a great deal of privacy. The bonus to all this is that almost everyone living in your dorm is in a similar situation. At times it can be awkward. Make an effort to meet as many people as you can. If your dorm or floor has a kick-off program or party, take the opportunity to get to know everyone. Introduce yourself and welcome others who make an attempt to befriend you.

If your RA holds meetings about campus or dorm safety, make certain you attend. In addition to receiving great safety information regarding your specific campus, it's another opportunity to make new friends. If you begin to feel lonely, call home, instant message an old friend, or get involved in a campus club. Keep busy.

Not in My Dorm

I know it's a shocker. Make no mistake, living in the dorms can be a blast! It can also be fraught with danger. It may even be deadly. Bad things happen to students every day in campus dormitories, including assaults, fires, rapes, and deaths. So how can you protect yourself and enjoy living in the dorm without becoming neurotic? It may sound trite, but prepare yourself. By simply understanding the mechanism of how crimes and accidents happen, you are better able to prevent it from occurring in the first place.

Simple common sense precautions may just save your life or the life of another student. No, you are not expected to become the dorm safety geek, walking around with a pen and clipboard making notes as you traverse the halls. But you have a responsibility to learn basic preparation skills and become familiar with your surroundings. As you are walking through the halls, make mental notes where the fire exits are located. Find the fire alarms and fire extinguishers. Do it regularly, and it will become second nature.

Let's be realistic, even the most stringent security measures can be bypassed if someone wants to get into your dorm bad enough. Just don't make it easy for them. Cooperation with dormitory security policies, the RA, campus police, and school officials regarding dorm safety is paramount. I promise you, there are people in your dorm who do not have your best interests in mind. If you think something is odd or someone looks suspicious, do not hesitate to call campus security or at least notify your RA.

Propping exterior dormitory doors open is a problem on many, if not most, college campuses. If you see an exterior door propped open, close it immediately. So it's just a propped door, what's the big deal? On April 5,

1986, a dormitory door was propped open at a residence hall in Lehigh University. Freshman Jeanne Clery was beaten, raped, and murdered in her dorm room by another Lehigh student attempting to commit a robbery. The perpetrator entered the dorm through a propped door. Jeanne's parents discovered that there were thirty-eight other violent crimes at Lehigh in the three years before Jeanne was murdered; however the students were never informed about the crimes.

Connie and Howard Clery, Jeanne's parents, connected with other campus crime victims. They lobbied Pennsylvania lawmakers to require colleges to publicize their crime statistics, and in May, 1988, Pennsylvania Governor Robert Casey signed the bill that made it law. On November 8, 1990, President George Bush signed a similar bill. After a few amendments, the Jeanne Clery Disclosure of Campus Security Policy and Campus Crime Statistics Act became federal law. The Clery Act, as it is known, is a federal law requiring all colleges and universities that participate in federal financial aid programs to keep and disclose information about crime on and near their campuses.

Security on Campus, Inc., is a nonprofit organization founded by Mr. and Mrs. Clery in 1987. It's an incredible organization "dedicated to safe campuses for college and university students." Their website, www.security oncampus.org, provides detailed information, up-to-date news regarding campus crime, crime statistics, and training seminars. No other organization in the country has done more to reduce college campus crime.

To give you some perspective, a *few* statistics demonstrate the unacceptable and overwhelming levels of crime being committed on campuses throughout the country. In 2004 alone, there were 3,680 sexual assaults; 48 murders; 5,915 robberies; 7,076 aggravated assaults; 21,859 drug arrests; 2,333 weapons possession arrests; 39,740 burglaries; 1,244 arson arrests; and 50,642 liquor law violation arrests. These numbers were taken directly from the Department of Education website. (Go to www.ed.gov and click on "Administrators" then "Safe & Drug Free Schools.") They are only a small sampling of actual overall numbers. They do not include accidents, Spring Break incidents, and crimes that occurred off campus. Additionally, these numbers include only those crimes that are actually reported.

Not all of these crimes happened because of a propped door. However, having one door propped open truly puts you and the entire dorm at risk.

Dorm crime can be broken down into two categories: incidents against the person and incidents against property. Since we have already touched on how crimes can affect the person, let's discuss crimes against your property. Everyone wants to make their dorm room their home. It's decorated with personal mementos and belongings that can be rather expensive and tempting to someone who may not have your welfare in mind.

Thieves today are no different than they were twenty years ago. They're opportunity seekers. If you give them the opportunity to steal something, they will. By reducing the criminal's opportunity, you reduce your chance of becoming a victim. Stereos, TVs, VCRs, DVDs, wallets, purses, and cash are very inviting to those who want to pull a quick caper. The two hottest items for theft? You guessed it: laptops and iPods. If you set them down, even for a few minutes, they *will* be stolen!

So what to do? First and foremost, do not give crooks the opportunity. Although it's common to leave your door open when you and your friends are together, get in the habit of locking the door when you leave. Even if you buzz down the hall for a moment or run to the restroom, lock your door. Almost all thefts in campus dormitories are the result of students leaving their doors unlocked. If your desk can be locked, lock it when you are not around. It's also imperative to keep all windows locked. If your dorm room is on the first floor or ground level, take extra precaution to lock your windows when you leave or are sleeping. If your room is secure, the thief is moving on to an easier target. I know, it sounds too easy.

Make a master inventory list of all your valuables, or anything you think is valuable. Ideally, this should be done prior to going to college. If not, make the list in your dorm and mail a copy home. As you're making the list, write a description of the item along with the serial number and model number. Note any identifying marks or scratches, and take photos if possible. With expensive items, you are strongly urged to engrave them with your driver's license number. Most colleges have an engraving tool for you to borrow. Call the security office and ask to sign it out. They will be more than happy to help you.

You will be in the bathroom longer than it will take for someone to grab a few goodies from your room. Colleges are not responsible for your belongings, so leave family heirlooms, expensive jewelry, or important items at home. Here are additional safeguards.

✓ If possible, engrave your belongings prior to arriving on campus.

✓ Consider placing a small mark on your belongings and take a picture of the item showing the mark.

✓ Engrave items with your driver's license number, *not* your Social Security number.

✓ Make a master list of all your belongings with a complete description of each item. Keep a copy of the list with you and keep a copy of it at home. Consider registering your list with the campus police department.

✓ If anything you have is stolen, no matter how small it may be, contact the campus police department.

✓ Your books are like cash—protect them.

✓ If you leave school for the weekend or break, take the time to secure most of your belongings out of sight. If possible, do not leave any valuables behind.

✓ Register your bike and write down the make, model, and serial number. Also, take a picture of your bike.

✓ If something doesn't *seem* right, or someone looks suspicious in your dorm, let your RA know immediately, or call 911.

✓ Never loan your room key to anyone.

✓ Always lock your door when you are sleeping.

✓ Never put notes on your door telling someone you are not in.

✓ Do not overload or cram an elevator, even if some students want to horse around.

✓ Make sure you have a working flashlight.

✓ Don't put your name on the outside of your dorm door.

✓ If someone comes to your room to do a repair, ask to see ID or call the front desk before you let them in. If a maintenance person does enter, leave your door wide open and stay with him or her until the repair is complete.

✓ Put your car keys on a separate ring from your dorm keys.

✓ If you are responsible for taking out your own trash, do so during daylight hours.

✓ Once your room is set up, take pictures of everything. This will help you recall items in the event they are missing.

✓ Be aware of who is taking your picture at a party in the dorms. It may end up on the Internet.

✓ Be aware of video cameras in your dorm.

✓ Get in the habit of showering when others are in the building.

Record Your Expensive Items.

	Item	Serial #	Model #	Value
1.				
2.				
3.				
4.				
5.				
6.				
7.				
8.				
9.				
10.				

✓ Try not to do your laundry late at night if the laundry is in the basement. Consider splitting a load of laundry with a friend. It is safer when others are around and will save you a few bucks.

✓ Be aware of voyeurs, or peeping toms in your dorm.

✓ LOOK OUT FOR EACH OTHER.

Insurance

"If students were to add up the cost to replace all the items in their dorm room, they would be surprised to learn the value," says State Farm Insurance spokesman Jeff McCollum. Do you have the extra cash to replace everything you own in the event something happens? Depending on your belongings and your specific situation, your agent may recommend a small renter's insurance policy. They are very inexpensive. For about twelve dollars a month, you could cover twenty-five thousand dollars worth of property and receive liability coverage.

Be very direct with your agent and ask if specific items are covered. Will my laptop be covered if it's stolen? Will my iPod be covered if it's stolen? Ask if your laptop is covered in the event you spill a cup of coffee in it. What about other electronics? With the cost of books, will my books be covered if my backpack is stolen? What is the process to file a claim? What is my deductible?

In most cases, as long as you're living in the dorm, you may not need a separate renter's insurance policy. You should be covered under your parent's homeowner's policy; however, circumstances may be different in each case. It's essential to check with your insurance agent prior to moving into the dormitory.

✎ Hot Tip:
Call your insurance agent *before* you leave for college.

Do not loan your keys or door access card to anyone. If you lose them, notify security immediately so your lock or key card can be changed. I know you're a kindhearted soul, but don't hold the door open for someone you don't know. If they live there, they should have their own key. Sooner or later, someone will ask, "Hey, do mind signing me in? I'm going to see Jeff on the second floor." Don't sign anyone else in, especially if you know the person doesn't live there. Tell him or her you can't, but that you will happily run to the second floor and get Jeff. By the way, what is Jeff's room number? According to the University of South Florida's Counseling Center for Human Development, 35 to 75 percent of all rapes against women are committed by men who know their victims. The very person you allow into your dormitory could become a major problem for you or someone else. Use common sense.

With the advent of social networking websites like Facebook, MySpace, and Badjocks.com, some students post their entire schedule online. Bad idea! You are telling a potential stalker your every location. You are also telling a potential thief, "I'm out of the dorm for a few hours, so now is a good time to clean out my room." Get in the habit of telling your roommate where you are by leaving a note, or write on an in-room chalkboard when you expect to return.

Could There Really Be a Fire?

Identify *exactly* what is outside your dorm window and how far down it is to safety. If you're hanging around one day, ask yourself, "What if?" How do I get out of here if something happens? Think this is extreme? Think again! The Center for Campus Fire Safety reported that 1,700 fires occur annually on college campuses throughout the United States. Although cooking, using candles, and overloading electrical outlets are major causes of fire in college dormitories, the leading cause is arson, according to Underwriter Laboratories (UL).

Many residence halls throughout the country don't have automatic fire sprinkler systems installed. At the time the buildings were constructed, fire sprinkler systems were not required under the building codes of the era. Today, any new residence hall will have fire sprinkler systems in place, and many states have already passed legislation requiring residence halls to be retrofitted with the systems. Considering that the cost of retrofitting older buildings is prohibitive, the time frame for doing such work will be many years, if ever. It's imperative that you consider fire safety while living in any campus dormitory.

✓ Do you know where *all* the exits are in your dorm?
✓ Do you know where the fire extinguishers are located?
✓ Do you know what is outside your window and how far down it is to safety?
✓ Does your room have a smoke alarm?
✓ Does your floor or hall have a smoke alarm?
✓ Are the hallways and stairs clear of belongings and debris, including bikes and boxes?
✓ Have you counted the doors to the nearest exit?
✓ Could you tie enough bed sheets together to break your fall if you had to use the window?

As in many emergency situations, every second counts. That is never more true than when dealing with fires, especially dormitory fires. When you hear a fire alarm, there is no way of knowing if the alarm is false. Get out of the building immediately. Do not delay! Your response to fire alarms must be automatic, every time . . . day and night.

Consider the following personal account.

JANUARY 19, 2000, SETON HALL UNIVERSITY

It was 4:30 a.m. Actually, I was awake, which was interesting. I had just woken up but I was reading. I got a telephone call from one of the priests who lived in Boland Hall who said there was a fire there. I asked him if it was serious and he said, "I think you should come over right away."

I was living in a residence for priests. I'm about a two-minute walk from Boland Hall and got over there right away. When I first got there, I realized that it was more serious than I wanted it to be when I saw the amount of fire equipment there and arriving. I did not see much smoke because the fire was confined to a sitting area or lounge area of the hallway. The fire got up to a couple thousand degrees. It melted a phone off the wall, but the room next to it was untouched. There was a lot of smoke damage along the hallways. I didn't see much, but there were students coming out of the building, and it was very clear there was a lot of damage to life. I immediately asked the fire chief when I got there if all the students were all right. The chief told me, "We don't know."

About twenty minutes after I arrived, the fire chief came out and said, "Monsignor, we have identified two students who are deceased, who have died in the fire." Shortly after we found out about the first two students, I was informed there was a third student who died. The world stops! It's a student that has died. Things will never be the same again. A fire is a tragedy, but a loss of life is a loss of life and it's forever. I just knew that the loss was immense. The magnitude of the fire was clear; the building was not going to burn down. But what became clear was that there was loss of life. I also saw a student who was very seriously burned. I just knew that the implications in terms of human loss and suffering were immense.

I would tell students to be careful and obey the rules. Sometimes there is a fire alarm, and students are brought out of the building at 2 a.m., and then you realize it was dust that got caught into the mechanism. Anyone who touches a fire alarm will be expelled immediately, and we will try to prosecute them criminally as well. Make sure administrators know the rules and enforce the rules. You can't have a thousand rules for young students. But the rules you have, you better enforce and enforce in a way that you know is for their safety. Seton Hall is committed to the safest environment possible. Safety is just presumed here at Seton Hall University; students breathe it. The bottom line is that a tragedy is a tragedy, and you never bring students back, and you can never take that grief away from the families. Students need to understand the Seton Hall story.

Monsignor Robert Sheeran, PhD
President, Seton Hall University

Boland Hall, a Seton Hall University residence in South Orange, New Jersey, was no different than any other freshman dormitory in the country. It housed hundreds of students from diverse backgrounds. The building, which remains standing, is divided into two structures. South Boland was built in the 1950s and North Boland in the 1960s. Although the building did not have sprinkler systems, it was completely within code regulations on that fateful night in January 2000.

On a bitter cold winter morning, around 4:30 a.m., most students were asleep. The fire alarms in Boland Hall began to wail. Many in the dorm were immune to the sound and dismissed it as another false alarm. With eighteen false alarms in five months, another alarm sounding was just an annoyance, especially in the middle of winter. There was only one difference between this alarm and all the others . . . this was real. Boland Hall was on fire.

Two students had set a banner on fire as a prank, and it ignited three couches and engulfed the room. Thick, black, choking smoke began to fill the hallway just down from where the fire started in the third-floor lounge. While most students evacuated the building, some were forced to jump from their dorm windows. Others still slept. Dana Christmas, an RA on the third floor could have left the building, but she didn't. Realizing students still were sleeping, Dana began pounding on the doors and yelling for students to wake up and exit the building. Dana saved countless lives that morning, but at a terrible cost. She was severely burned over 60 percent of her body.

In the aftermath, three Boland Hall students were killed, fifty-eight were injured, and hundreds of lives would be altered forever. After years of investigations, the two students accused of setting the fire pleaded guilty to arson and were sentenced to prison.

Almost eight years after the fire, the president of Seton Hall reflected on that day. "If there is a positive effect from this, it is Seton Hall is a much stronger, more tightly and closely knit community now than we were before the fire. There was a dramatic difference. It's like families who experience a tragedy, they are different. The tragedy doesn't go away, but somehow they are bound together."

More than likely, your dormitory will have false alarms. It will also have fire drills. I implore you to take every alarm seriously. If you hear a fire alarm, do not wait until smoke and fire are present before you evacuate the building. When you are in any building, if you notice a fire alarm, fire hose, or fire-detection system that is broken or out of place, notify your RA or security immediately. Tampering with these devices is illegal.

There are many things you can do to prepare yourself in the event a fire occurs. Become very familiar with every aspect of your dormitory. When you leave for class one day, consider taking the stairs. Count how many flights of steps there are to an exit. Memorize the number of doors from your room to the nearest exit. If your room does have automatic sprinkler systems, never hang anything from the sprinkler heads or piping. If your individual room does not have exclusive smoke alarms, purchase one. They are about the same price as a burger and fries. Install new batteries at the beginning of each semester.

Always know two ways out of the building. Walk both routes a few times each month, and it becomes second nature. Besides, the exercise is good for you. I realize you are aware of the dangers fire presents, but many of these simple suggestions and precautions can mean the difference between life and death. Take a minute to reacquaint yourself with these safety measures.

- ✓ Never ignore any fire alarm!
- ✓ Think! Every second counts.
- ✓ Your number one priority is survival. You must do whatever it takes to survive.
- ✓ If you have a disability, let your RA know before you begin your dorm stay.
- ✓ Locate multiple exits in either direction from your room.
- ✓ Call 911 *after* you leave the building.
- ✓ Before opening the door, touch the doorknob. If it's hot, the fire is close, and the door should remain closed. Try to put wet towels around the door to block smoke. If you have a window, try to make an exit from there or get the attention of people on the ground.

✓ If smoke is present, stay low, about one foot off the ground. Smoke, toxic gases, and heat rise. Crawling on the floor will keep you under the smoke.

✓ If you are able to get out of your room, yell "FIRE!" as you are leaving, and pull the fire alarm if you pass one.

✓ Pull your door closed when you leave your room.

✓ Never go back into the building unless you are given the all-clear signal.

✓ Do not call anyone before you leave. Get out first and make a call once outside.

✓ Do not grab your belongings. Just get out of the building.

✓ If you are unable to leave your room, hang a sheet or something from the window to alert people that you are there.

✓ Have an idea of what you could use to tie together such as sheets, clothes, and comforters in the event you have to exit your window.

✓ If you're unable to get out of the building, and it's a large building with windows that do not open, do whatever you have to do to break them open and get someone's attention. Use a chair or some metal object to break the glass.

✓ Do not use the elevator during a fire; use the stairs.

In addition, consider appliances that have an automatic shutoff, so they aren't accidentally left on all day. Keep curtains away from hot surfaces and open flames such as candles. Never leave a burning candle unattended. Do not leave flat irons or curling irons unattended. Never smoke in bed.

There may come a time when you see a small fire. If your laptop battery caught fire or your trash can, would you know how to properly use a fire extinguisher? Learn how to use a fire extinguisher before it is necessary. There is an mnemonic acronym for using fire extinguishers.

P = Pull the pin.

A = Aim the extinguisher nozzle at the base of the fire.

S = Squeeze or press the handle.

S = Sweep at the base of the fire from side to side.

I'm Not an Electrician

"Everybody come out quick and look at the lights!" Those words were said by Chevy Chase, a.k.a. Clark Griswold, in the classic 1989 movie *Christmas Vacation*. No sooner had Clark plugged in the outside Christmas lights, than the overloaded circuit blew out power to the entire town. I will promise you this, you will have more devices and appliances with plugs than available outlets to accommodate them. A quandary for sure, but don't panic.

According to the Electrical Safety Foundation International, www. electrical-safety.org:

Electrical safety is quite simple. Treat anything that plugs in as if it were an employee with a grudge—willing to work, but awaiting its chance to zap you. Liquid and electricity don't mix; don't introduce them. Heating appliances (toaster and microwave ovens, hotplates, hair dryers, popcorn poppers, irons, coffee makers) use more electricity and are more likely to cause overloads than things that don't heat. If your school allows these, use special care. Even a small motor in a fan or a mixer is probably stronger than your fingers. Stop it and unplug it before you stick your hands in it.

Many residence halls were built years ago, before every student arrived with a computer, CD player, microwave, refrigerator, wireless telephone, halogen study lamp, fan, and fax machine. Dorm wiring simply cannot handle the electrical load. And despite the tuition, your college isn't made of money. Wasting electricity costs the school a lot and adds to pollution.

Before you begin your dorm-room-wiring job, assess the appliances you have and the available outlets. Now, take into consideration your roommate's devices. Together, you've got a lot. More times than not, you will need power strips. You should have received something from your college or RA outlining what type of extension cords and electrical power strips are approved. Follow the instructions specific to your particular building. In the event you did not receive any information, consider these suggestions to keep your room free from electrical hazards.

✓ Purchase power strips with an over-current protector. Power strips with an over-current protector shut off power automatically if there is too much current being drawn.

✓ Never overload electrical outlets, extension cords, or power strips. If they become hot, unplug them immediately and notify your RA.

✓ Use caution in older homes or apartments. Their wiring may not be modernized and may be unable to handle the amount of electricity needed if multiple power strips are used.

✓ Most dormitories do not allow halogen lamps. If they do, they must be designed with a mesh guard that prevents contact with the bulb. Halogen lamps can reach over 900 degrees.

✓ Typically, toaster ovens are not allowed either. These appliances can become so hot, they can easily burn you if you touch the exterior.

✓ Make sure light bulbs are the correct wattage for your lamp.

✓ Never cut off the grounding pin from a three-pronged cord.

✓ Never use a frayed wire or extension cord. This is a problem waiting to happen.

✓ Do not staple extension cords to your wall or desk.

✓ Don't throw clothes on top of extension cords or any wires.

✓ Do not route cords under doors or carpet.

✓ Never drape clothes, towels, or any type of fabric over lamps.

2

My Safe Campus

Whether your college is located in an urban or rural setting, this small square-mile area will be your home for the next four years. It is where you will live, study, play, and work.

While every campus in the country differs, there are still many similarities. You will walk to class, walk to other dorms, walk to the cafeteria, go shopping, attend sporting events, go to restaurants or bars, and study at the library, just to name a few. Even if you are fortunate enough to have a car on campus, you will still spend most of your time walking. Each day can present a different challenge. You will walk in rain, sleet, snow, and heat. Couple the above with walking at night, and the entire safety outlook changes.

College campuses are no different than any other town in America. There are problems and crime. Unfortunately, with tree-lined streets and cute boutiques, many students tend to let their guard down. It's almost as if they are lulled into a false sense of security. Many problems can be prevented, however, by employing basic common sense precautions that can significantly reduce the likelihood of being attacked or hurt on campus.

The goal in any new environment is to develop a level of comfort with your surroundings. Problems can arise anytime, anywhere—whether you're enjoying a country picnic lunch or a night on the town. There is a delicate balance, however, between being totally on edge and becoming overly complacent and careless. Become comfortable, while being attentive to your surroundings.

As you are walking or driving on campus, stay alert. Be observant. If you are using an iPod, one of your most important senses is occupied—your hearing. Make sure you continue to look around and walk with confidence. Listen to your instincts. The suggestions in this chapter are essential precautions that can considerably reduce the chances of your being attacked or hurt on campus. Here are a few general rules:

✓ When you walk on campus, walk with confidence. Stand up straight, look directly at people, and make eye contact.

✓ Try to walk with someone else. Make it a point to notice who is leaving your class and heading in your direction, either to the dorms or your next class. Chances are they will welcome your company.

✓ Make sure you know the exact location of the outdoor emergency phones on campus.

✓ Never use an iPod while walking at night.

✓ Do not take the same route every day. Switch your routine.

✓ Walk on the sidewalks whenever possible. If you have to walk on the street, do so facing traffic.

✓ Know the phone number for campus police.

✓ Let your roommate or friends know your schedule. Chances are they'd like to give you their schedule as well.

✓ Be sure the paths you take have decent lighting and are well traveled.

✓ If you have an evening class, walk back to your dorm with a partner.

✓ If you are waiting to get on an elevator and the person standing with you is making you feel uncomfortable, do not get on the elevator.

✓ Keep the phone number for the campus escort service with you at all times.

✓ If someone stops and asks you for directions, do not approach the car. Maintain a safe distance between you and the people in the vehicle.

✓ Avoid taking shortcuts, especially at night. Yes, you may save two minutes, but you could be inviting problems.

✓ If you are driving on campus, always look for parking spaces that are well lit.

Every now and then, as you are walking to class, think of "what if" situations.

✓ What if someone was following me at this location on campus? What would I do?
✓ Where is the closest emergency phone?
✓ What store, restaurant or building is available for me to ditch into?

Now, attempt the same scenario at the same location when you're walking at night. Notice how different things appear in the evening. Observe the trees and bushes. Note the lack of people. Would you respond in another way? Are you a bit on edge, and do you feel a sense of nervousness because it's dark outside? That's good. It will make you more cautious.

I'll Take a Café Mocha

And I'll take your laptop, thank you very much!

No one enjoys a café mocha more than yours truly. (Decaf, extra hot, no whip please—just in case you're wondering.) I know that hanging out in a coffee house can be relaxing. Whatever you do, though, secure your belongings. Bring them with you to the restroom if you must. To be fair, I am not just picking on coffee houses. The criminal element can be anywhere, both on and off campus.

If someone robs you or holds you up and wants your money or some personal belongings, by all means hand them over. No amount of money or *stuff* is ever worth getting hurt over. Use caution if you're carrying large amounts of cash or wearing expensive jewelry. Every day on college campuses students have property stolen. Don't set yourself up to become a victim. Make certain that someone you know and trust is watching your valuables or don't leave them unattended. Your possessions will disappear faster than it takes you to grab a cup of coffee.

When you're buzzing around on campus, try to keep all your belongings in one backpack. Keep in mind, though, that backpacks are an easy target. Never leave yours unattended. If someone does grab it, he'll be hard to recognize with your backpack slung over his shoulder. You will never find him.

When I was a kid one of my favorite programs was Mutual of Omaha's *Wild Kingdom* with the legendary Marlin Perkins narrating suspenseful stories of wild animals from around the globe. I learned at a very early age that when animals in the wild search out prey, they look for easy targets. They will hunt for an animal that has roamed from the pack, and they will search for animals that look weak.

The same holds true for criminals. Whether they're thinking about stealing your iPod or contemplating an attack, criminals are searching for easy targets. By not making yourself an easy target and by demonstrating confidence, you significantly reduce the likelihood of becoming a victim. You typically do not hear about criminals walking up to a crowd of people and saying, "Hey, you with the brown hair. Come over here so I can steal your laptop." No, the crook will wait. He will linger around until he catches you off guard, and then he will pounce.

Depending on the college you're attending, you may see campus police in cars, on bicycles, and on foot. Schools with larger campuses have large police departments with officers on duty to "protect and serve" twenty-four hours a day, seven days a week, handling thousands of calls per year. A campus police department's presence is not intended to relieve you of taking personal responsibility for your own safety, however. The safest campus environment exists when a partnership is formed between the police and the students, with everyone respecting the security measures set up for your protection. Get to know your campus police. If you have a few minutes, stop and introduce yourself.

You can also assist police by being observant. If you happen to witness a crime on campus, no matter how small it may be, take the time to report it. Call campus police or 911 and tell them what you witnessed. Try to give them a description of the person or at least the direction they were heading. Chances are your tip will aid them in other investigations.

The Phones in the Bright-Colored Boxes

Almost every college and university has emergency telephones strategically placed throughout their campuses. These phones are great, and you should not hesitate to use them. Colleges mark the emergency phones in various bright colors from yellow to blue, orange, and red. Some phones or call boxes will have a blue or red light on top of the box, and all you have to do is pick up the receiver inside. A dispatcher will answer the call, and an automatic signal will be sent so police will know your exact location on campus. As you are walking to class or visiting a friend on the weekend, make it a point to know where these phones are located. If an uncomfortable situation arises, by all means use the campus phone.

Campus Stalking

The United States Department of Justice defines stalking as, "A pattern of repeated and unwanted attention, harassment, contact or any other course of conduct directed at a specific person that would cause a reasonable person to feel fear."

According to the National Center of Victims of Crime (NCVC), "Stalking victimizes more than one million women and nearly 400,000 men in America each year." From following you, to making obscene phone calls, and from e-mailing you unwanted computer images to texting your phone, stalking on college campuses is serious and can take many different forms. Stalking could also include someone waiting for you outside your dorm or apartment, sending you unwanted gifts, or even vandalizing your property. Should you ever feel you are being stalked, notify campus police immediately. Also, consider these suggestions.

- ✓ Listen to your instincts. Your gut feeling may be correct.
- ✓ Keep a detailed record of the incidents as they happen. Write down dates, times, and locations. If you are able, jot down the color of the stalker's clothes and describe any person who may have witnessed the episode. It is important to make this record as soon as time permits, while the event is still clear in your mind.

✓ Let your roommate, friends, and family know that you suspect you are being stalked. Keep anything the stalker sends you for evidence. For example, print e-mails, save cards and letters, write down phone numbers as they appear on your caller ID.

✓ Try to save any voice-mail messages. Keep cell phone bills for records.

✓ Have your phone set up so that someone must "unblock" their number in order to contact you. Now you will have a record of the call.

✓ Try to get a picture of the person. Most cell phones today have cameras. Use caution, but let the person know that you just took his picture, and you'll be informing the police if it continues.

✓ Be very direct and tell the person to leave you alone.

✓ Call campus police and file a report.

Get Walking or Driving Escorts When Necessary

I doubt they will take you to the mall whenever you want, but a college escort service may take you around campus. Most large colleges and universities have these services available, and you will be informed prior to arriving at school if this wonderful service is provided. Jot down the shuttle service phone number right away, and keep it with you at all times. Take note of the hours and any requirements as well.

Walking escort services can be staffed by police or students who are cleared by campus security. They will assist you and your visitors if you feel unsafe walking alone. The escort services are not just for females. Male students can and should ask for an escort if they are uncomfortable for any reason. These folks are happy to help you and are staffed for your convenience.

A Quick Stop at the ATM

Just as you and your friends are running out the door on a Saturday night, it dawns on you that you have six bucks to your name. No problem, you figure. You'll head to the ATM real fast and grab twenty dollars to tide you over. It's 9:45 p.m. as you pull your car up to the window of the ATM, located on the edge of the bank's parking lot. Just as you enter your PIN, a guy appears out of nowhere, shoves a gun in your face through the open window, and says, "Gimmie your money, now!" Completely freaked out, you step on the gas and make your way out of the bank's parking lot. Even though your card is still in the machine, you get away unscathed. You were lucky—this time.

Random acts of violence can occur at any time and any place, and ATMs are no exception. By taking a few precautions at any type of ATM, whether walk-up or drive-through, you reduce your chances of becoming a victim.

- ✓ Try not to use an ATM after dark. If you do, make sure the one you are using is in a well-lit area.
- ✓ Try to use an ATM inside a bank or in a building on campus.
- ✓ Whether driving or walking, ask one of your friends to come along with you.
- ✓ Many ATM machines are in the back of the bank, near the parking lot. Try to avoid these machines if possible.
- ✓ If driving to an ATM and someone is in front of you using the machine, put enough space between the vehicles so you can avoid being trapped.
- ✓ If you are ever robbed at an ATM, don't worry about giving the robber your pass code. Most banks limit the amount you can withdraw per day.
- ✓ Limit your time at the ATM. Have all your information ready to go before you arrive for the transaction.
- ✓ Never count the money while you're standing near the machine or sitting in your car. Once your cash is withdrawn, take your card, receipt, and money, and put them in your pocket immediately. Even if the machine did make an error and dispense the wrong amount, there is nothing you can do about it until the bank reopens.
- ✓ If you are using a drive-through ATM, make sure your doors are locked and all windows closed except the one you are using. Be alert at all times. Look to the front, sides, and rear of your car, and keep your vehicle running. If someone approaches your car, cancel your transaction and leave immediately.

✓ Drive as close as possible to the ATM, while using caution not to hit the machine. Doing this can make it more difficult for someone to get between the car and the machine

✓ Once you pull in or walk up to the ATM, if you feel you were followed, leave immediately and call 911.

✓ If people are behind you, even in daylight, block the view of the machine as you are using it so they do not see your code. Take your receipt because most show your available balance.

✓ Be alert as you approach the ATM for loiterers or a suspicious-looking person in a car.

Me, Defend Myself?

Choosing whether to submit or defend yourself is very tricky. Often resistance can be a dangerous course of action, and you should never feel guilty if you submit to the attacker's demands.

Because no two situations are the same, let's at least explore some options that you may have available. Clearly, if you feel that you could be hurt worse by fighting back, don't! Attackers may become enraged. Perhaps there's a chance that you could talk your way out of it. Lie if you must. Tell him anything you have to, if you think it may prevent the attack. Consider acting your way out of it. Act as weird as you possibly can. Anything goes! Start with something as simple as saying, "My roommate will be home in minutes." Or, "Look, if I go out with you again, will you stop?" But if he stops, call the police when he leaves. Then there are more drastic actions like trying to make yourself vomit or peeing in your pants.

How you defend yourself should be based on whether he has a weapon. Nothing is worth dying over. If you can escape, do not attempt to fight this guy. Your goal is to get away and put distance between you and the attacker. It is an assessment that only you can make. If you do not have a chance to make a move right away, try stalling him for an extra few minutes, another opportunity may come along. If you feel the time is right, make your move. This is not a time to be gentle. Unleash whatever power you can muster and aim for vulnerable areas.

✓ Shove your finger directly in his eye.
✓ Kick or grab his groin.
✓ With your heel, step hard on the top of his foot.
✓ Bite whatever you can get a hold of—his ear, his nose, or his fingers.

Again, you are just doing this to give yourself a few precious seconds to escape. Ten or fifteen seconds may be all you need to put some distance between you and the attacker. Notify campus police, or call 911 immediately. It may be hard, but do your best to get a good description of the person. Did you notice the color of his shirt or pants? Was he wearing glasses? What's the color of his hair, etc.?

Many college campuses offer the Rape Aggression Defense System, or R.A.D. class to their students. This program is discussed in detail in Chapter 3. Check to see if R.A.D. or something similar is offered at your school. Contact your campus police department and inquire if any self-defense courses are offered. You need to know how to defend yourself.

A Horrific Day

On April 16, 2007, the deadliest shooting in United States history took place on the campus of Virginia Tech, in Blacksburg, Virginia. By day's end, a crazed gunman had killed thirty-two students and teachers and wounded twenty-five more. This unspeakable tragedy devastated the entire college community and their families.

It was not the first time such a tragic event has occurred where students gather to learn. On April 20, 1999, two students entered Columbine High School in Littleton, Colorado, with a cache of weapons and homemade bombs. When their shooting rampage was over, twelve students and a teacher would die before the gunmen committed suicide. On August 1, 1966, a student at the University of Texas at Austin shot and killed fourteen people and wounded thirty-one others. The gunman targeted his victims from the observation deck of the Main Building tower.

Following the Virginia Tech tragedy, President George W. Bush said, "Schools should be places of safety and sanctuary and learning. When that sanctuary is violated, the impact is felt in every American classroom and every American community."

Governors throughout the country immediately formed task forces to review safety on America's college campuses. College and university administrators began to reevaluate their school's ability to notify the student population if such a catastrophic event occurred again. While all this transpired, advocates on both sides of the gun issue took the opportunity to debate their positions.

College campuses are open to the public and therefore not easily safeguarded. Similar to a large mall or any public shopping area, installing fences and metal detectors are impractical solutions. Mass notification systems that would instantly communicate a message to the entire student body are being considered by university officials throughout the country. In June 2007, Virginia Tech installed such a system.

While I cannot conceive any method that would completely prevent another tragedy of this magnitude from happening, there may be measures that students can consider if they are present while an active shooter is on campus. Due to the tragedy at Virginia Tech, many colleges and universities have posted suggestions on their websites in the event shots are fired.

I asked Dr. Jason Winkle, PhD, the current president of the International Tactical Officers Training Association, for his suggestions for protecting yourself from an active shooter. He is the Director of Combatives at the United States Military Academy, a martial artist with twenty-two years of experience, and he holds instructor rank in seven martial arts systems. Dr. Winkle has trained members of the United States Special Forces, as well as numerous law enforcements agencies. He teaches close quarters combat, close quarters battle tactics, hostage-response tactics, and vehicle assault and vehicle ambush defense. He instructs college and high school administrators on active shooter situations. He is also assistant professor of physical education at Indiana State University. Simply put—Dr. Winkle is the best there is!

Here are some of Dr. Winkle's insights into active shooter situations.

THE TRUTH ABOUT AN ACTIVE SHOOTER:

✓ The average active shooter situation lasts seventeen minutes.
✓ Most victims are shot within the first three minutes of the incident.
✓ Active shooters are spontaneous.
✓ Active shooters are unpredictable.
✓ Active shooters choose target-rich environments.
✓ First responders are typically outgunned and not properly trained.

Depending on where you are in relation to the shooter, and the shooter's posture, your appropriate course of action may vary. The following is easily said, but not easily done; try not to panic and use common sense.

IF YOU ARE OUTSIDE IN AN OPEN AREA

If you hear what you believe are shots, try to make a determination where they are coming from. You obviously do not want to walk toward the shooter. Is the shooter walking around firing at will or is he stationary?

✓ Find appropriate cover: a building, a wall, a large tree, or a parked car.
✓ Stay low. Make your profile as small as possible.
✓ If the shooter is walking in your direction, run from the area if the opportunity presents itself. If you do run, go in a zigzag pattern. It's very difficult for an untrained person to hit a moving target.

IF YOU ARE IN A CLASSROOM

Quickly determine what resources you have available in the classroom to either block the door or escape: desks, file cabinets, and windows. You are trying to buy time for police and SWAT to move in. Active shooters want to do maximum damage, so they tend not to waste time working to get at victims. Rather they will move on to a more vulnerable target.

✓ Stay in the room. Lock-down and barricade the classroom door with anything that is on hand. The heavier the object, the better the door will be barricaded. Possibly drive a wedge under the door, too.

✓ If the classroom door has a window, cover it if possible; use paper, a shirt, or a jacket.

✓ Move students to an area of the room that is out of the line of fire from the doorway, and stay very quiet.

✓ If the shooter continues to try to enter the room, and you feel exiting a window is the best option, by all means do it. Be very quiet as you exit, so you do not indicate what you are attempting.

FACE-TO-FACE WITH A SHOOTER

No one can properly prepare you for a face-to-face encounter with a gunman. Only you can make a determination to take measures to save your life. If the gunman is not shooting, do exactly as he says, and do not make sudden moves. If shooting begins, you must make choices. Try to run, stay and do nothing, consider attacking the shooter, or play dead. These decisions are unnerving, but you need to become as creative as possible to survive. If police or SWAT officers see you, do *exactly* what they tell you and respond quickly. Police have no idea who you are!

Just Going Out for a Run

Lord knows I *should* go for a run, but I have bad knees. Really! If you're a jogger or like to go for an occasional run, make sure you are familiar with the area and know the route prior to departing. If you are going to jog by yourself, let someone know your exact route. Better yet, ask a friend to come with you. It's certainly much safer to run during daylight hours. If you do find yourself jogging in the evening, make sure your route is well lit. No matter what time of day you head out for a run, keep these additional safety tips in mind.

✓ Always let someone know you've gone for a jog. Leave a note with the time you departed, your route, and expected time you should return. If your plans change while out on your run, call your room-mate and let her know; borrow a phone if necessary.

✓ Wear bright clothing to improve visibility.

✓ Never jog near heavily wooded areas.

✓ Be extra cautious if you use an iPod while jogging. Consider turning the volume down or removing one of the ear buds.

✓ Carry or wear a lightweight whistle.

✓ If you are jogging on the street, face traffic.

✓ If you think someone is following you, change directions and cross the street.

✓ If you enjoy jogging at night, consider purchasing a blinking light that can be strapped to your arm. They are relatively inexpensive and can be purchased at most sporting goods stores.

If riding bikes is your passion, many of the same precautions should be observed, though there are a few important additions:

✓ Ride your bike on the righthand side of the road. Go with the traffic.

✓ Always wear a helmet.

✓ Obey all stop signs and traffic lights.

✓ If you ride your bike in the evening—to and from class or for plea-sure—make sure you have a white light in the front and a red light or a reflector in the back. Consider installing a blinking LED red light on the back of the bike. They are not expensive and can be seen for miles.

✓ Know the hand signals to indicate turns and stops.

✓ Remember, although you can see the cars, it may be difficult for drivers to see you. You are a much smaller target.

At some large urban colleges, you may occasionally come across pan-handlers. Of course the choice is yours if you care to reach out and help these folks, but use caution. The safest thing to do is politely say no and keep walking.

Commuting

With college costs escalating every year, more students are finding commuting to school an attractive alternative. Some students find they are better equipped to focus on their studies while staying in a familiar, comfortable atmosphere like their home. Above and beyond the obvious financial considerations, there is a great deal to be said for commuting. Chances are you're less likely to get into trouble. Roommates are not an issue; nor is the noise factor in the dorm. There is no packing, unpacking, and moving to worry about. Or perhaps you have a great job and would like to retain your seniority within the company.

Commuting is a personal decision. Whatever your reason for commuting, consider these suggestions for making your commute as safe and efficient as possible.

✓ Drive around campus prior to the start of the school year to familiarize yourself with the campus.

✓ Know where you are allowed to park.

✓ Make sure you have all the appropriate stickers or window tags on your car or you may receive a parking ticket.

✓ Select the best route to campus prior to leaving. Also, make sure it is a safe route.

✓ Have an alternate route planned prior to the beginning of school. Take this alternative a few times to make sure you're comfortable with it. You can bet that construction will be going on or an accident will happen the day you are running late for a test.

✓ Make sure you have enough fuel in the tank.

✓ Have you ever changed a flat tire? The day you are taking mid-terms is not the best time to learn how. Make sure you can handle a jack and have flares available. Before school begins, jack up your car and try to change the tire.

✓ Consider joining AAA or some other reputable road service in your area.

✓ Use caution in rush-hour traffic.

✓ When approaching stoplights, do not pull up to the bumper of the car in front of you. If you do, you will be sandwiched in. Give yourself enough space so you are able to pull out if you have an emergency.

Don't Mess with Mother Nature

EARTHQUAKES

Any campus in an earthquake prone area will have very specific safety instructions should Mother Nature act up. Your university may have evacuation and assembly areas for each building on campus. Depending on the quake's magnitude, the shaking can become quite violent. If you live on or near a fault line, it is advisable to have an earthquake survival kit. Understanding the hazards from an earthquake can lessen your chances of becoming injured. Follow some of these safety tips in the event an earthquake strikes.

✓ Seek shelter immediately under a desk or a table. Try to protect yourself from falling objects. Ceilings, light fixtures, and overhead lights can fall during earthquakes.

✓ Stay clear of windows and overhead lights. Windows will easily shatter and send glass flying in all directions.

✓ If you are inside without the possibility of cover, stay low and keep tight against an interior corner wall. Cover your head and face as much as possible.

✓ Never use elevators during or directly after an earthquake. Take the stairs.

✓ If you are lying in bed when an earthquake strikes, protect your head with your pillow.

✓ If you are near a doorway, use it for cover only if you know it is supported very well, preferably a load-bearing doorway.

✓ If you are in a store when an earthquake strikes, take extra caution. Most stores have hundreds of overhead lights and shelves stocked with merchandise. Products on shelves can become missiles. Cover your head and try to make your way to a wall.

✓ The electric service may go out, fire alarms may sound, and fire sprinkler systems may activate even though there is no fire.

✓ If you are already outside, head to an open area. Move away from buildings, trees, and overhead wires.

✓ Earthquakes are known for rupturing gas lines. There is a good chance natural gas is leaking. Do not smoke, light matches, use lighters, or be near any open flame.

✓ Use caution exiting buildings as debris can fall just outside of doorways.

✓ As soon as the earthquake is over, exit the building immediately.

✓ If people are seriously injured, do not move them unless they are in grave danger from the building collapsing or burning.

✓ Be prepared for aftershocks. More than likely, they will happen and can still cause damage.

✓ Never re-enter the building until it has been inspected and given an all-clear.

EARTHQUAKE SURVIVAL KIT

Families living on or near known fault lines should have extensive emergency supply kits. Most students would not have the need for such a kit, but there are many that do. In the event that your college is in a known earthquake prone area, there are a few things you should consider. Formulate a communication plan well in advance with your family. Let them know that you will contact them after the quake. Keep a small box on hand outfitted with basic necessities.

✓ Flashlight with new batteries
✓ Portable radio with extra batteries
✓ Enough bottled water and canned food to last a couple of days
✓ Manual can opener
✓ First aid kit
✓ Extra clothes, shoes, blankets, and money

TORNADOES

"Toto, I've got a feeling we're not in Kansas anymore." That was the memorable line Judy Garland, a.k.a. Dorothy, said to her dog Toto after a tornado picked up their house and dropped it in the magical Land of Oz. Tornadoes are nothing to mess around with. Just ask Toto.

Tornadoes can occur in any state and are considered one of nature's most violent storms. Their destruction can obliterate entire towns. Unlike hurricanes, many tornadoes strike with little or no warning. Areas in the Midwest, Texas, and Florida are especially susceptible to tornadoes, but any town that is experiencing violent thunderstorm activity could encounter a tornado. Most colleges and universities will have procedures in place should a tornado warning be issued. The National Weather Service and your local television station will issue tornado "watches" and "warnings."

A tornado watch:

Means given the current weather pattern, there is a chance of a tornado being formed. Stayed tuned to your local radio or television station for updates.

A tornado warning:

Means a tornado has been spotted or detected on radar. Find shelter immediately.

Towns and colleges where tornado activity is prevalent will use sirens as a warning system. It is extremely important to familiarize yourself with your campus's tornado warning system. Chances are if you attend college in a tornado-prone area, the sirens will sound. Understand these procedures as soon as you get to campus and find out where the recommended shelter is located. Depending on the severity of the storm, if a tornado warning is given and there are weather spotters on the ground, the spotters may issue a tornado rating. The rating system, called the F-Scale, was named after Dr. Tetsuya Theodore "Ted" Fujita, a University of Chicago meteorologist.

F-0: Light damage –	Wind speed	below 73 mph
F-1: Moderate damage –	Wind speed	73-112 mph
F-2: Considerable damage –	Wind speed	113-157 mph
F-3: Severe damage –	Wind speed	158-206 mph
F-4: Devastating damage –	Wind speed	207-260 mph
F-5: Incredible damage –	Wind Speed	261-318 mph

The Federal Emergency Management Agency (FEMA) lists the following facts about tornadoes.

✓ They may strike quickly with little or no warning.

✓ They may appear nearly transparent until dust and debris are picked up or a cloud forms in the funnel.

✓ The average tornado moves southwest to northeast, but tornadoes have been known to move in any direction.

✓ The average forward speed of a tornado is 30 mph, but may vary from stationary to 70 mph.

✓ Tornadoes can accompany tropical storms and hurricanes as they move onto land.

✓ Waterspouts are tornadoes that form over water.

✓ Tornadoes are most frequently reported east of the Rocky Mountains during spring and summer months.

✓ Peak tornado season in the southern states is March though May; in the northern states, it is late spring through early summer.

✓ Tornadoes are most likely to occur between 3 p.m. and 9 p.m., but can occur at any time.

In Your Dorm or Other Buildings

If you're inside when a tornado warning is issued, stay inside. If you're in a large structure like a gymnasium, church, or store, find an interior bathroom or a small closet area that is clear of any windows and glass. Also, follow these precautions:

✔ Move to the lowest level of the building.
✔ Stay clear of any windows at all costs.
✔ Go to a center hallway if there's no basement.
✔ Get under a desk or table.
✔ Cover yourself with a mattress or sleeping bag.
✔ Stay away from exterior walls.
✔ Try to get into a small room like a closet or bathroom.
✔ Position yourself under a stairwell.
✔ Crouch as low as possible and cover your head.
✔ Lay in a bathtub if one is near.
✔ Never get on an elevator.
✔ Never go outside until an all clear is given or the warning has expired.

I'M OUTSIDE; NOW WHAT?

If you're outside as a tornado approaches, try to make your way to a building. If you are unable to seek refuge, consider these tips:

✔ Move as far away as you can from trees and cars.
✔ Try to find a low-lying area.
✔ Lie flat with your face down.
✔ Cover the back of your head with your arms.

I WAS JUST DRIVING ALONG

Being in any vehicle when a tornado is nearby is extremely dangerous. If you can see the tornado, and it's still far away, you may be able to drive out of its path by moving at right angles away from the tornado. Only attempt this if traffic is light and the tornado is far in the distance. Never try to out run the tornado! If a tornado is nearby, exit the car immediately and attempt to find a sturdy building. If no building is available, move away from your car, lie face down, and follow the steps above.

HURRICANES

On August 29, 2005, one of the deadliest and costliest hurricanes in the history of the United States slammed into the Gulf Coast. The category 5 hurricane killed at least 1,836 people and cost over 81 billion dollars in damage. Hurricane Katrina's wrath left a path of destruction so widespread its effect will be felt for decades. Although not all hurricanes are that catastrophic, their damage can be devastating to property and life.

Fortunately, with advanced radar, hurricanes are detected many days before making landfall. Either watches or warnings will be issued in the event a hurricane may pose a threat. While only a portion of the United States is affected by hurricanes, millions of college students are on campus during hurricane season. The Atlantic hurricane season is from June 1st through November 30th.

A hurricane watch:
Means hurricane conditions are *possible* in the specified area of the WATCH, usually within 36 hours.

A hurricane warning:
Means hurricane conditions are *expected* in the specified area of the WARNING, usually within 24 hours.

It is of utmost importance to monitor NOAA Weather Radio or your local television and radio stations for instructions. Your school will have very specific instructions if you are advised to evacuate. As always, stay indoors and away from windows.

3

Would You Like to Go Out Tonight?

It's Friday night. After three different outfits and two ways of doing your hair, you and your girlfriends are ready to go out dancing and enjoy a few drinks. You're having a great time chatting with your friends at a local bar when you notice a couple of cute guys standing at the table next to yours. The guys strike up a conversation, and the one you're talking with asks you to dance.

It appears you're hitting it off, and he tells you he knows of a great party across campus. Why not? you think. It sounds fun and appears to be innocent enough. As you're walking across campus, you begin to tell each other *your story*, where you're from, why you chose your school, and what you are majoring in.

You arrive at the party where everyone is dancing and having a great time. Your new guy draws you a beer from the keg and introduces you to his friends. After a few pleasantries, you start dancing the night away. You're happy. This is college life. What a fun night!

The time is ticking away, and it's now 2:00 a.m. You mention to your date that it's getting late and that you're ready to go home. Being the gentleman he is, he offers to walk you back to the dorm. You arrive in the lobby, and you both agree that it was an enjoyable evening. He informs you he's having a little get together at his apartment on Saturday night, and he would love for you to be there. After you give him your phone number, he kisses you on the cheek and walks out of the dorm lobby.

Tired, but excited, you head to your room. Your roommate is still awake chatting with the friends you began your night with hours earlier. They're all dying to know about your night, and the questioning begins. How was it? What happened? Where did you go? Is he nice? He is so cute! Does he have any friends?

During the interrogation from your friends, you tell them all about your new guy. "He's so nice. He comes from a great family. His dad is a doctor and has written a book. He's a finance major and would like to get his MBA. He's such a gentleman. I'm going to see him tomorrow night." It is now 4:00 a.m., and you go to sleep.

At 12:15 p.m. you get out of bed. You missed breakfast at the cafeteria, but you figure if you throw sweatpants on right now and hustle you can make the last twenty minutes of lunch.

As you walk back from the cafeteria you suddenly realize it's only eight hours before your date arrives, and you have nothing to wear. Panic sets in because you know you don't have the extra money to shop for new clothes. Your roommate, being the kindhearted person she is, loans you her new miniskirt and matching top. She'll not be wearing them this weekend because she's going home for the night to get a home-cooked meal and catch up on laundry.

At 8:00 p.m. your date phones and tells you he'll pick you up within the hour. You hurry with the last bit of make-up and right on schedule he calls and says he's in the lobby. Your date gives you a quick kiss, tells you that you look great, and you both begin the short fifteen-minute walk across campus to his apartment.

Once there, you begin to feel comfortable with his friends and their dates. You are enjoying a few glasses of wine, eating some snacks, and getting along well with everyone. One of the guests at the party suggests you play *quarters*, a drinking game on campuses for decades. Sure, you think, why not? You are in control and besides, you don't plan on drinking too much.

It's around midnight, and you have a nice buzz going. Everyone is giggling and laughing and truly having a wonderful time. You begin to slow down drinking because you know that you are becoming just a *little* intoxicated, but you don't stop. The classy guy that your date is notices you have had too much to drink and suggests to everyone aloud, that he better take you home before you get completely smashed.

You appreciate the fact that he's watching out for you, and without hesitation, you say goodbye to everyone and make your way back to your dorm. Feeling very comfortable that his intentions are nothing but honorable, you invite your date up to your room. Once inside your dorm, you put a CD on and begin to laugh and reminisce about his silly friends and the party you just left.

Your date reminds you that you're lucky he got you out of there when he did because his roommates can play drinking games all night long. Feeling grateful for his help, he pulls out the bottle of wine that you were drinking earlier and suggests you both have a quiet glass together before he returns to his apartment. Not sensing anything is amiss, you reach for two glasses and get comfortable on the couch.

After fifteen minutes, you begin to feel very drunk. It's almost as if you are dreaming. You know that you've had a few drinks, but you can't understand why you're feeling so intoxicated. Your nice date, the finance major, the doctor's son, the guy you met less than thirty hours ago, just slipped you a date-rape drug and is about to rape you repeatedly over the next few hours.

Although dating on campus is a natural part of the college experience, this chapter could be troubling for some to read because so many women are sexually assaulted. According to the Rape, Abuse, and Incest National Network—RAINN, every two and a half minutes, somewhere in America, someone is sexually assaulted. One in six American women are victims of sexual assault. RAINN also estimates that 59 percent of sexual assaults go unreported.

According to the University of South Florida Counseling Center for Human Development, 90 percent of all rapes and sexual assaults that do occur on campuses go unreported. They also conducted a nationwide study on college campuses that revealed the following:

✓ 35 to 75 percent of all rapes against women are committed by men who know their victims.

✓ 52 percent of women students have experienced some form of sexual victimization.

✓ 1 in 8 college women have been victims of rape.

✓ 1 in 12 college men admitted to sexually abusing women but did not consider themselves rapists.

✓ 47 percent of rapes were by first or casual dates or by romantic acquaintances.

✓ Over one-third of the women didn't discuss the rape with anyone, and over 90 percent didn't report it to the police.

Although the numbers in the above studies differ regarding the amount of sexual assaults that go unreported, they are both extraordinarily high. Due to the number of women who become victims, most colleges and universities across the county offer sexual assault awareness programs. You are strongly urged to participate in these programs if they are available. The programs are popular and often fill to capacity. Check with your school regarding the times and locations of available programs on your campus.

Whether walking across campus, enjoying a party with friends, or spending time alone with a date, women must take precautions to reduce their chances of being sexually attacked or raped. It can happen at any time and in any location. Preparation is paramount. Before you walk out of the door, visualize where you are going. Train yourself to become more safety conscious. If you intend to drink alcohol, know your limit before you depart. Here are some protective measures to follow if you're walking in a variety of settings.

✓ Don't automatically trust anyone you meet. Trust must be earned!

✓ Be aware of your surroundings at all times.

✓ Always walk with confidence.

✓ Never walk alone at night.

✓ Always travel on well-lit roads.

✓ Listen to your instincts. If you even *think* you're being followed, cross the street and walk in the opposite direction.
✓ Make direct eye contact with people you see or meet. If someone is just hanging around, look them directly in the eye.
✓ If you do stop and talk with someone, maintain a safe distance between you and the person with whom you're talking.
✓ Tell your friends your schedule and the approximate time you will return.
✓ Always have a charged cell phone in your possession.
✓ Carry a whistle or some other device that can make a loud noise.
✓ Consider carrying mace or pepper spray. This is an individual decision, but make certain that you are proficient using a weapon of this kind. Also know this could be used against you in the event of an attack.

Sexual Assault

It's still a misconception that most rapes occur from the attacker lurking in the bushes or in a parking garage. While it's certainly true that these types of attacks occur, the majority of sexual assaults are committed by someone who is known to the victim. The 2005 National Crime Victimization Survey revealed that 73 percent of sexual assaults were perpetrated by a non-stranger; 38 percent of perpetrators were a friend or acquaintance of the victim; 28 percent were an intimate, and 7 percent were a relative.

Sexual assault is anything that forces an unwanted act that is sexual in nature. Sexual assault is a crime. It includes inappropriate touching, child molestation, rape, attempted rape, and any type of sexual intercourse—vaginal, anal, or oral—that you say "no" to. Sexual assault can happen anywhere and can be perpetrated by anyone.

But I Like This Guy . . .

Perhaps, but proceed with caution. No one is suggesting that you bring an entire entourage of security personnel on your date. However, you can take steps to protect yourself. You could double-date for a while until you become more familiar with him. If double-dating is not your style, suggest a movie or dinner at a restaurant instead of having dinner in his apartment. Control the situation. Let him know that you're controlling the date. If he begins to balk, let him know from the outset that you intend to move slowly. Chances are if this guy likes you, he will be more than happy to accommodate your recommendations and respect your wishes.

Don't let him convince you to go anywhere you're not comfortable going. Try to stay in public places as much as possible. Get in the habit of limiting the time you spend alone with a date. If he becomes frustrated that you're not alone enough on the first date or two, this may be a red flag. Ask yourself from time to time, "How well do I really know him?" Trust cannot be assumed! Just because your date went well the first few times, doesn't mean it's going to go well the next time you get together. Keep your guard up.

Be very clear with anyone you date or spend time with regarding your sexual boundaries. I understand it may be difficult while in the midst of a sexual encounter, but only do what you're comfortable doing. "NO" means no! It's not up for interpretation or debate! While no one can completely protect themselves from every form of assault, there are certainly steps you can take to minimize your risk.

✓ Try not to go to unfamiliar areas when you begin dating a new person. Give your roommate, or someone else you trust, as much information as possible about your date. Write down his name, phone number, and any address you have. Let your friends know where you plan on going.

✓ Always carry your own money. Never let a date tell you that you owe him. You owe him nothing.

✓ If you ever feel uncomfortable about anything, get out of the situation. Lie if you must, but do everything you can to eliminate the problem.

✓ Never leave a public place with someone you just met.

✓ Never accept a drink from anyone you don't know.

✓ Never ever leave your drink unattended. Take it to the restroom if you have to.

✓ Be confident in your principles regarding sexual activity. Do not feel pressure to have sex.

✓ Just because you have sex once with a guy, it doesn't mean that he is entitled to sex again.

✓ Every situation is different. If it begins to become threatening, you must do whatever you can to prevent or survive an attack. That may include trying to get away, fight, or submit to your attacker.

✓ Never feel guilty if you are the victim of an assault of any kind.

It Takes Two . . .

Guys, allow me to give you an example. If I come to your house on a Sunday afternoon to watch a baseball game, does that mean that I am automatically invited back every Sunday for the rest of the baseball season? If I am invited to your house for the game, does it mean that I am entitled to stay longer for dinner and dessert every time I come over? Of course it doesn't. Consenting to one thing does not mean you will be agreeable to the same thing in the future.

The same analogy can be applied to females. If you are engaged in a romantic encounter with a particular girl, it doesn't mean that you're automatically entitled to do anything with her again. If you have sex with a girl once, it doesn't mean that she's willing to have sex with you in the future. Ever! Just because you are passionately kissing a girl, and she is enjoying it, does not entitle you to go any further. Like it or not, the call is hers.

Although the majority of this chapter is focused on protecting women, I am also trying to look out for you. There are quite a few terms associated with this topic, and each one has a slightly unique meaning: sexual assault, date rape, acquaintance rape, and attempted rape. Whatever your interpretation is, they are all still crimes. I will leave it up to the psychologists why sexual assault occurs at such an alarming rate, but there are some facts that guys need to understand. If you commit any of those actions, there is a good chance you are going to jail or, at minimum, you are going to be convicted of a sex crime.

It's really quite simple. A perceived lack of communication is no defense. If you're drunk, it's no excuse, even in a court of law. If she's intoxicated, and unable to tell you "No," you could be charged with rape if you have sex with her. Regardless of what you think a girl means, or how she is acting, you cannot assume anything. Being charged with sexual assault or rape can affect you forever. Can you afford for that to happen?

Remember when you were a child, and you walked into a store with your mother, and she would say, "Ask before you touch anything." If that is what you must do with your date, then do it. Take nothing for granted. As a male, you also need to protect yourself. There should never be a grey area. The following suggestions are meant to be a guide for you to eliminate any confusion.

✓ "NO" means no! It's not up for interpretation or debate!
✓ Do not pressure or coerce girls to have sex or ask them to go any further than they are comfortable.
✓ Just because you have had sex in the past with your date doesn't mean that you're entitled to have sex with her in the future.
✓ If you're engaged in any sexual activity and she changes her mind and says, "No," you must stop immediately.
✓ Being drunk is not an excuse for pushing sex.
✓ If you're unsure how the girl feels about having any kind of sexual contact, stop what you are doing and ask.
✓ If she does not verbally tell you to stop and begins pushing you away, you must stop at once.

Adding to the staggering sexual assault numbers in the past years are date-rape drugs. Alcohol is considered the most widely used date-rape drug available. Although there are many variations of date-rape drugs on college campuses, the term usually applies to three drugs: GHB (or gamma-hydroxybutyrate), Rohypnol, and Ketamine hydrochloride.

A date rape drug is any drug or any substance that is colorless, odorless, and tasteless, which when given to someone causes severe impairment. Many of these drugs are used to spike drinks. Spiking a drink is when a foreign substance is slipped unknowingly into someone's drink. This can be done anywhere, but is commonly done at parties, bars, and dormitories. Date-rape drugs are virtually undetectable and will make a victim unable to resist a sexual attack. Most date-rape drugs are fast-acting and will leave the victim with little or no memory of the attack. They can completely incapacitate a person for up to eight hours.

Date Rape and Predatory Drugs

Date-rape drugs, or predatory drugs, as they are sometimes called, are any drugs that can be used to assist in a sexual assault. They include alcohol, marijuana, sleeping pills, cocaine, and even cold medicine. As discussed, the drugs most often associated with date-rape drugs are GHB (or gamma-hydroxybutyrate), Rohypnol, and Ketamine hydrochloride.

Alcohol: Without a doubt, alcohol is the most common date-rape drug there is. It is legally sold in all fifty states, it's inexpensive to obtain, and most victims usually take it willingly. Additionally, depending on the amount consumed, alcohol will act as a sedative, will cause you to lose some degree of inhibition, and will cause varying degrees of amnesia. If alcohol is combined with other date-rape drugs, it can be a potent and sometimes lethal recipe for disaster.

GHB: Gamma-hydroxybutyrate (GHB) is an expensive, colorless, odorless drug that is typically sold as a liquid but may be found in powder form. You could taste this drug if consumed by itself, but when mixed with a drink it becomes virtually undetectable. The drug is also called Liquid Ecstasy, Easy Lay, and Bodily Harm among others. This drug is long-lasting and will work shortly after ingested.

Project GHB, www.projectghb.org, is a watchdog group based in Mesa, Arizona. Founder Trinka D. Porrata, president of Project GHB, is a retired thirty-year veteran of the Los Angeles Police Department, Narcotics Division, and is a nationally and internationally recognized expert on GHB and other predatory drugs. Porrata said, "People don't understand that GHB is easily obtainable. It is a clear liquid that looks just like water. It's typically put in small plastic bottles."

GHB is highly addictive and produces a high or euphoric feeling as inhibitions are depressed, according to Project GHB. The most distinctive and terrifying feature of GHB is its overdose time course. Within fifteen minutes, a person's state of mind becomes altered, and there is a high possibility of a loss of consciousness or an actual coma.

Rohypnol: Pronounced "row-hip-nol," this drug also goes by the street names—Roofies, Mexican Valium, R-2, and Trip and Fall. Rohypnol is a sedative similar in size and shape to an aspirin. The small white tablet is commonly compared to Valium. However, according to www.drugs.com, the online provider of drug information, "Rohypnol's sedative effects are approximately 7 to 10 times more potent than Valium."

Manufactured by Hoffman-LaRoche, this drug is illegal in the United States. While it's against the law in America, the drug is legal in more than fifty other countries where it is used to treat insomnia. Even though the drug is illegal, it's easily obtained and very inexpensive. According to the U.S. Drug Enforcement Administration, Rohypnol is usually smuggled into the United States by mail or delivery services.

As a predatory or date-rape drug, Rohypnol will dissolve quickly in most beverages. It is colorless, odorless, and tasteless. However, if dissolved in alcohol, Rohypnol could have a bitter taste. The U.S. Department of Health and Human Services states that the new form of the pill will turn blue when added to liquids. However, the old pills are still available.

The sedative effects of Rohypnol cause confusion, sleepiness, a drunken feeling, loss of muscle control, and amnesia. The drug can take effect within twenty to thirty minutes and may last between eight and twelve hours.

Ketamine Hydrochloride: Pronounced "kee-ta-meen," this drug is sold under the brand names Ketalar and Ketaset. Sold legally in the Unites States, Ketamine is a white powder used mostly on animals as a veterinary sedative.

It's also used for human consumption in hospitals as an anesthetic. Street names for Ketamine include Kid Rock, Special–K, Super–K, and Vitamin–K.

Ketamine can be snorted or smoked and added to marijuana or tobacco. Primarily, Ketamine is slipped into a drink and given to the unsuspecting victim. If not administered properly by a healthcare provider, Ketamine can be extremely dangerous. It may cause hallucinations, convulsions, problems breathing, aggressive or violent behavior, memory problems, and lost sense of time and identity. Many other negative side effects could occur as well. Ketamine takes effect in as little as ten minutes and lasts up to three hours.

SO HOW CAN I PROTECT MYSELF?

First, understand that these drugs are readily available to those determined enough to acquire them. There's no question that it's frightening to think that you could fall prey to a date-rape drug, but there are precautions you can take. Start practicing the following behaviors as soon as you arrive on campus your freshman year. If you make slight adjustments to the way you handle beverages, these practices will soon become habits, thus decreasing the probability of becoming a victim of a date-rape drug.

- ✓ Never leave your drink (alcoholic or nonalcoholic) unattended, even for a second. Take it with you to the restroom if you must.
- ✓ Don't turn your back on your drink, even while you're sitting at a table.
- ✓ Never accept a drink from anyone you don't know.
- ✓ If in a bar or nightclub, try to get your drink directly from the bartender. Don't have someone in your party get the "next round" and then leave the group and walk alone to the bar.
- ✓ While in a restaurant, only accept drinks from the waiters or waitresses.
- ✓ If someone offers to buy you a drink, walk with them to the bar and don't take your eyes off the drink. Never let a stranger purchase a drink for you.
- ✓ Watch your friends. If they appear "too drunk" for the amount of

alcohol they have consumed, get them away from the situation, and don't leave them alone. Should they become incoherent or act in a strange manner, call 911.

✓ Never drink from open punch bowls or open common containers.

✓ Do not drink anything that tastes or smells strange. Sometimes GHB can taste salty.

I CAN TEST MY DRINK?

You can now test your drink thanks to a company called Drink Safe Technology. The company was founded in 2002 after a friend of the founder, Francisco Guerra, fell victim to a sexual predator. With the help of Scientific Coordinator Dr. Brian R. Glover, Drink Safe Technologies invented, after a year and a half of research, a patent-pending device that signals when a drink has been contaminated with two of the most commonly abused date-rape drugs, GHB and Ketamine.

There are two products available. One is called the Drink Spike Detector. About the size of a credit card, each Drink Safe card contains two tests. If the card comes in contact with GHB or Ketamine it will change color. The second product is a Drink Safe Coaster. A standard size coaster for setting drinks on, the Drink Safe Coaster contains two tests that will also change color if a drink is spiked with GHB or Ketamine. *Time Magazine* named the Drink Safe Coaster the 2002 Best Invention of the Year.

Drink Safe products are available nationwide at your neighborhood CVS Pharmacy. To order any Drink Safe products online, log onto www.drink safetech.com or call 1-888-707-7233.

✎ Hot Tip:
Drink Safe products make a great gift.

WHAT IF I AM A VICTIM?

The U.S. Department of Health and Human Services recommends the following suggestions if you think you may have been a victim of any date-rape drug. If you feel your roommate or friend has been under the influence of these drugs, be proactive and get them the assistance they need.

✓ Go to the police station or hospital right away.
✓ Get a urine test as soon as possible as the drugs leave your system quickly. Rohypnol stays in the body for several hours and can be detected in the urine up to seventy-two hours after taking it.
✓ Do not urinate before getting help.
✓ Do not douche, bathe, or change clothes before getting help. Your body and clothes may contain evidence of the rape.
✓ You also can call a hotline crisis center to talk with a counselor. RAINN—the Rape, Abuse, and Incest National Network—is the nation's largest anti-sexual assault organization. RAINN operates the National Sexual Assault Hotline and carries out programs to prevent sexual assault, help victims, and ensure that rapists are brought to justice. *Worth* magazine has called RAINN, "One of America's 100 best charities." Visit www.rainn.org or phone the hotline at 1-800-656-HOPE (4673).

The National Center for Victims of Crime (NCVC), www.ncvc.org, is the nation's leading resource and advocacy organization for crime victims. Since 1985, they have worked with more than 10,000 grassroots organizations and criminal justice agencies serving millions of crime victims. Phone: 1-800-394-2255.

The R.A.D. Systems

Taught to over 250,000 women, The Rape Aggression Defense System, or R.A.D., is "a program of realistic self-defense tactics and techniques for women. The R.A.D. System is a comprehensive, women-only course that begins with awareness, prevention, risk reduction and risk avoidance, while progressing on to the basics of hands-on defense training."

The R.A.D. Systems are free programs located on college campuses and via police departments throughout the United States and Canada. A listing of the Systems is as follows.

✓ **R.A.D. Basic Physical Defense:** The cornerstone of R.A.D. Systems, this course has its foundations in education and awareness. The course includes lecture, discussion, and self-defense techniques, suitable for women of all ages and physical abilities.

✓ **R.A.D. Advanced Self Defense:** Builds on techniques and strategies from the Basic class and adds defenses against the edged weapon and firearms. This program also covers more prone-defense strategies, multiple-subject encounters, and even low- and diffused-light simulation exercises.

✓ **Aerosol Defense Options:** Using the proven R.A.D. Systems philosophy, Aerosol Defense Options destroys the myths and manufacturer hype about pepper spray effectiveness and even their ability to deter a committed focused aggressor. Learn the most realistic methods for accessing, deploying, and assisting the aerosol defense option. If it fails to work, and it may, learn the proven backup strategies needed for successful escape.

✓ **Keychain Defense Options:** Continuing to enhance the many options of self-defense, this program is for the instructor who wants to put an impact weapon in the hands of the students they train. The R.A.D. Keychain Defense Options course is one of the only realistic and court-defensible impact weapons programs available for the general public. Combining proven R.A.D. Physical Defense strategies with revolutionary impact weapons defense techniques, makes this program a worthy addition to the R.A.D. System.

The R.A.D. Systems website, www.rad-systems.com, is a comprehensive site featuring everything that R.A.D. Systems has to offer. Click on the Program Locator link to find a program listed in your area.

4

Alcohol and Drugs on Campus

You've finally graduated high school, have attended a few parties over the summer, and have taken a senior trip with a few of your friends. You made it—you're in college. Freshman orientation is over, and you're living in the dorms. It's the end of August, and it's hot outside. The girls are lying on the lawn in their bikinis, and the guys are throwing the Frisbee on the Quad. It's great. It is your first weekend on campus. Let's drink!

As the afternoon progresses, the question of the day becomes, "Where are the parties tonight?" You discuss the options with your friends and begin to network with other students. You've learned that the bars have been tough to get into lately. They're closely checking identification. Since your fake ID has not yet been acquired, you decide it's best to find a party off campus. If all else fails, you know that your roommate's friend is twenty-one and will make a beer run for you to pick up a few cases. You're thinking, it is not a bad last resort, but you wonder, "How the heck do we sneak four cases of beer and ice into the dorm?"

At dinner you run into a few friends who inform you that they know of a huge party off campus. "It's a closed party, but we can get you in," they say. Fortunately, at least for right now, you don't have to worry about sneaking beer into the dorm. You will handle that problem at another time. After you receive all the pertinent information about the party, you and your friends finish dinner and make your way back to the dorm.

It's still warm outside, and on the way to your dorm, a couple of your high school friends are hanging outside their dorm window yelling at you, "Come on up." You have plenty of time before the party so you make your way up to their room. They're just lying around enjoying a few beers when they ask you if you know of anything going on tonight. You're feeling kind of privileged that you have insider information, so you're reluctant to say anything. But after a few beers, you loosen up and say, "Look, I shouldn't be telling you this, but we know of a party. It's a closed party, but we'll try to sneak you in."

At 9:30 p.m., you and your friends make your way across campus to the party. As you approach the door, you notice a guy sitting on a stool . . . collecting. "Three bucks for the guys, one buck for the girls," he bellows to everyone in line. The house is small and the party is packed. You look around and make your way to the bathroom where two half kegs are sitting in the bathtub full of ice. Someone is pumping the tap as you draw a large beer.

Around midnight, the already crowded house is now busting at the seams. Both kegs have been replaced by fresh ones, and there is no end in sight. You notice your roommate in the kitchen with lots of people around cheering him on. It's beer-bong time, and he has the hose. The funnel is filled up as he tilts his head in the ready position. The guy holding the hose releases his thumb as thirty-six ounces of beer is shot down your friend's throat in less than three seconds. With only minimum spillage down the front of his shirt, your roommate yells a resounding "Yeah!" as the guy with the beer-bong shouts, "Who's next?"

By 3:00 a.m., you and the group of friends you came with are more than drunk, you're boiled! After tripping and hanging all over each other you somehow manage your way back across campus to the dorms. Everyone goes to their respective building and crashes in their clothes. You and your roommate stumble upstairs and you both climb into your bunks. You think, "Oh man, what a fun night!"

At 6:35 a.m., there is a loud pounding on your door. Still technically drunk, and not sure what's going on, you open the door and there is utter chaos in the hall. Campus police, local police, paramedics, and firemen are scurrying around while at the same time drilling you with questions. Confused, and still unsure what is happening, you are told by your RA, "Your roommate is dead! He's in the bathroom and choked on his own vomit."

Without question, the number one problem for colleges and universities throughout the United States is alcohol. From freshman orientation through graduation, alcohol use on college and university campuses is constant. It's overwhelming! As a country and as a society, alcohol use is devastating. According to the Centers for Disease Control and Prevention (CDC), "There are approximately 75,000 deaths attributable to excessive alcohol use each year in the United States. This makes excessive alcohol use the third leading lifestyle-related cause of death for the nation. In the single year 2003, there were more than two million hospitalizations and more than four million emergency room visits for alcohol-related conditions."

As I mentioned in the introduction of this book, I am not here to tell you, "Do not drink." For me to tell you not to drink whether you are of legal age or not is meaningless. I understand that. I am also well aware that the message of underage drinking has been pounded home on multiple fronts. I would like to take a different approach. Throughout this chapter, you may notice that I quote many statistics. As you read the statistics, I ask that you give them more than a cursory read. Try to absorb them so you can appreciate the gravity of this out-of-control problem. I offer these numbers to you as evidence to substantiate the level of destruction that alcohol has caused on college campuses.

Using another analogy, I am going to assume that most of you have flown in an airplane. Whether you fly regularly or not, everyone has heard the flight attendant's message, "There are two exits in the front, two over the wings, and two exits aft." The message is not random. This message is given every time you fly. No exceptions! The flight attendant is not telling you how to crash the plane; she's teaching you how to respond in the event the plane crashes.

Similarly, this chapter is not designed to teach you how to drink. It's intended to teach you about the choices you have available and how to respond in situations when alcohol is present. This is a chapter about choices—personal choices, smart choices, safe choices, and sometimes life-altering choices. The choices you make regarding alcohol can have a direct impact on your life.

Too Many Choices

By the time you enter college, you will be making many decisions on a daily basis. Your parents are no longer around to guide you each day. Technically, you could call your parents and ask for their opinion, and occasionally you will need their input. However, college is a time for maturing. It's a time for you to grow and live by your own decisions, whether they're right or wrong. Some decisions may not be overly important, while others matter a great deal. "Do I get out of bed and go to the cafeteria for breakfast this morning?" "Should I take twelve credits and have a lighter schedule this semester or eighteen credits and get ahead for the year?"

You don't have to be on campus for a long period of time before you're faced with making decisions regarding alcohol. It's everywhere! You'll have to make decisions regarding alcohol even if you don't enjoy drinking it. More than likely, you'll gravitate towards students with similar interests, and alcohol may be one of those interests. There will be a desire to belong. Peer pressure is ubiquitous on college campuses, and there will be times when you must make a choice to either succumb to the pressure or hold strong.

Examine your own experience with alcohol. How many times have you consumed alcohol? Can you truthfully say to yourself that you know your limit and you know how your body is going to respond every time you drink? If you say yes to that question, then you're more experienced than most of the adults I know. Do you have the experience to gauge your limit? Each person is different, and every day is different. How much food have you recently eaten? How tired are you? Does your body react differently when you drink hard liquor? There are many variables when considering alcohol absorption rates.

For a moment, try to equate drinking alcohol with learning to drive a car for the first time. When you received your permit, did you jump in the car and begin to drive? Were you experienced enough to drive into the city and parallel park your first day behind the wheel? Would you feel comfortable driving in rush hour traffic or a snowstorm your second day behind the wheel? Would it be a smart choice to get behind the wheel of a high-performance car and drive in an ice storm? Would you let *your* child do it? Of course not!

Yet, every year on college campuses, many students will engage in a level of excessive drinking that is unprecedented in their lives. When you combine the lack of experience with high-risk drinking the consequences can be catastrophic—similar to driving the high-performance car in an ice storm.

The National Institute on Alcohol Abuse and Alcoholism, NIAAA, reported that excessive and underage drinking affects virtually all college campuses, college communities, and college students whether they choose to drink or not. Here are some of the consequences for college students between the ages of eighteen and twenty-four:

- ✓ **Death:** 1,700 college students die each year from alcohol-related unintentional injuries, including motor vehicle crashes.
- ✓ **Injury:** 599,000 students are unintentionally injured under the influence of alcohol.
- ✓ **Assault:** More that 696,000 students are assaulted by another student who has been drinking.
- ✓ **Sexual Abuse:** More than 97,000 students are victims of alcohol-related sexual assault or date rape.
- ✓ **Unsafe sex:** 400,000 students had unprotected sex, and more than 100,000 students report having been too intoxicated to know if they consented to having sex.
- ✓ **Academic Problems:** About 25 percent of college students report academic consequences of drinking, including missing class, falling behind, doing poorly on exams or papers, and receiving lower grades overall.
- ✓ **Health Problems/Suicide Attempts:** More than 150,000 develop an alcohol-related health problem, and between 1.2 and 1.5 percent of students indicate that they tried to commit suicide within the past year due to drinking or drug use.

✓ **Drunk Driving:** 2.1 million students drove under the influence of alcohol last year.

✓ **Vandalism:** About 11 percent of college-student drinkers report that they have damaged property while under the influence of alcohol.

✓ **Property Damage:** More than 25 percent of administrators from schools with relatively low-drinking levels and over 50 percent from schools with high-drinking levels say their campuses have a "moderate" or "major" problem with alcohol-related property damage.

✓ **Police Involvement:** About 5 percent of four-year college students are involved with the police or campus security as a result of their drinking, and an estimated 110,000 students are arrested for an alcohol-related violation such as public drunkenness or driving under the influence.

✓ **Alcohol Abuse and Dependence:** 31 percent of college students met criteria for a diagnosis of alcohol abuse and 6 percent for a diagnosis of alcohol dependence in the past twelve months, according to questionnaire-based self-reports on drinking.

The numbers above are devastating! Stop and think for a moment . . . 1,700 students die each year, just from alcohol. Thousands of families are devastated because of the poor choices their children made. The inexperience you have with alcohol can occasionally create miscalculations that are so destructive that they are life altering. If you make the decision to drink, ask yourself which category below you would fall under.

LOW-RISK DRINKER:

✓ You don't drink until you are twenty-one or older.

✓ You eat a full meal before having any alcohol.

✓ You have a plan on how you intend to get home before you leave for the evening.

✓ If you're a woman, you drink no more than one drink per hour; if you're a male, you drink no more than two drinks per hour.

✓ You never set your drink down and walk away.

✓ You switch between alcoholic and nonalcoholic beverages.

✓ You try to eat nonsalty food while you're drinking.

✓ You always set a limit on the amount of drinks you will have prior to leaving the house.

✓ You always request that someone watch out for you.

✓ You make certain that a designated driver is arranged prior to leaving home.

HIGH-RISK DRINKER:

✓ You're not too worried about having a designated driver.

✓ You rationalize that you are *okay* enough to drive after you have had a few drinks.

✓ You drink with the sole intention of becoming intoxicated.

✓ You participate in drinking beer-bongs, playing drinking games, and doing shots.

✓ You're not too worried about eating prior to going out.

✓ You rationalize that mixing alcohol and drugs, including prescription medications, is not that much of a concern.

✓ You don't mind following the crowd.

Numbers to Reflect Upon

According to the U.S. Department of Education, in 2003, there were 48,115 arrests on college campuses for liquor-law violations. In that same year, there were 161,974 disciplines on college campuses for liquor-law violations. The number of alcohol-related arrests and disciplines is almost twice the number of all other college-crime categories combined.

What's interesting about these numbers is they only tell *part* of the story. The numbers above don't include on-campus alcohol-related "accidents" and off-campus alcohol-related accidents and crimes. For example, each year almost two-million college students travel to various resort areas for Spring Break. Thousands of students are either arrested or injured because of alcohol use; some are killed. The number of students hurt on Spring Break due to alcohol is not included in the Department of Education's tally.

Nor do the numbers include most off-campus alcohol incidents— the type that happen at off-campus fraternities and sororities and night-clubs. We've all heard the news reports about a college student who has mysteriously vanished after a night of partying only to be found deceased weeks later.

What the Heck Is Binge Drinking?

So your friends drink a lot, does it mean they're binge drinkers? Possibly. Ask ten experts to define binge drinking for you, and you're likely to receive ten different answers. Some consider a binge drinker to be a person who is drunk daily and who seems to disappear while on his drinking marathon. Others believe binge drinking is when a male consumes four drinks in two hours, and a woman consumes three drinks in two hours—or enough to bring a person's blood alcohol content to 0.08 grams or higher. Different countries have very different definitions.

Let's keep in mind the college perspective—a definition most students can relate to. Binge drinking college style: a person who drinks a lot of alcohol in a short amount of time so he can get drunk. Simple! The bottom-line, binge drinking is extraordinarily dangerous. It can take many forms—from drinking numerous shots of liquor in a row, consuming one beer after another, playing drinking games, and doing beer-bongs.

Let's talk about beer-bongs since they appear to be a favorite at many college parties. Some beer-bongs hold sixty ounces of beer, or five twelve-ounce beer cans. When the valve is opened, five cans of beer will shoot down your throat in just over three seconds. Now there's a smart choice that will make you proud. In case you're wondering, yes, I did time it.

Work with me here, we're still on beer-bongs. Everyone has a comfort zone. For most of us, it's something we don't even notice. It's more of a subconscious process we go through in most of the activities we do. What *you* may feel comfortable doing, someone else may not.

For instance, probably somewhere in your town, there's a neighborhood with a posted speed limit of 20 mph. I would venture to say that most of you would be comfortable driving a few miles an hour over the posted speed limit, say 23 or 24 mph. However, I doubt anyone would be comfortable driving 60 mph through the same neighborhood. The notion of driving 80 mph in a 20 mph zone is ludicrous.

Even the most irresponsible of students would not drive 80 mph in a 20 mph zone. They know it's extremely dangerous. They also know that if they don't kill themselves or someone else, there's a very good chance they'll be in a great deal of trouble if they get caught. They understand the consequences! Doing beer-bongs and binge drinking is similar to driving 80 mph in a 20 mph zone. The only difference is most students don't understand the consequences or the incredible danger they put themselves in. Just because you see students doing beer-bongs does that mean it's a safe activity?

I Just Want to Have a Few Beers

If that's your choice, then be safe about it. In no way do I condone underage drinking or excessive drinking of any kind. However, I am a realist. The precautions and suggestions in this section are intended to lessen your chances of becoming injured while drinking.

✓ Under no circumstances should you drink and drive.

✓ Always plan *before* you go out for the evening. Plan how you're going to get to the party, and plan how you're going to get home.

✓ Make sure you eat a full meal before you begin to drink.

✓ Make sure you have a friend with you.

✓ If you feel any peer pressure to drink, make up an excuse. Any excuse! "I've been sick, I'm taking medication, I'm getting up early, I need to study first thing in the morning, or I'm the designated driver for the night." If the pressure continues, leave the party.

✓ Continue to snack on foods while you're drinking.

✓ Drink in moderation. Remember, you just went out for a few beers.

✓ Always carry the number for your local cab service in your purse or pocket.

✓ Avoid walking home along the side of the road.

✓ Never, ever leave your friend alone in a bar or an apartment with someone she just met. Tell her anything you have to, but don't leave her with a stranger! Every year, the media reports on students who have vanished after a night of partying, only to be discovered deceased days later. There is no question it can be difficult. You would like to return home, and your friend wants to stay a while longer. Try to convince her not to stay, or consider remaining with her until she leaves.

✓ LOOK OUT FOR EACH OTHER!

What Is My BAC?

BAC stands for Blood Alcohol Content. Simply put, it is the amount of alcohol in your blood. There are many factors to consider when determining BAC percentages including your weight, how much food is in your system, whether you are male or female, and how quickly you have consumed alcohol.

The alcohol impairment guides featured below are meant to be a guide and not a guarantee. They were provided by the Pennsylvania Liquor Control Board, Alcohol Education department. For the purposes of the chart, the PA-LCB clarifies that "one drink" is equal to the following:

✓ 1.5 ounces of 80 proof liquor or distilled spirits
✓ 12 ounces of regular beer or
✓ 5 ounces of table wine

If police stop a suspected drunk driver, he may be given a field sobriety test. These unofficial tests are used as a guide to determine if further testing is required. Some of these tests may include walking a straight line, standing on one leg, and closing your eyes and touching your nose with your finger. If a person fails that test, he may be asked to submit to a breathalyzer test. The breathalyzer is used to estimate your BAC. Chewing gum, eating breath mints, or even biting an onion will not mask or lessen the effects of

ALCOHOL IMPAIRMENT CHART

NEVER DRINK AND DRIVE

APPROXIMATE BLOOD ALCOHOL PERCENTAGE

Drinks	Body Weight in Pounds								
	100	120	140	160	180	200	220	240	
0	.00	.00	.00	.00	.00	.00	.00	.00	ONLY SAFE DRIVING LIMIT
1	.04	.03	.03	.02	.02	.02	.02	.02	Impairment Begins
2	.08	.06	.05	.05	.04	.04	.03	.03	
3	.11	.09	.08	.07	.06	.06	.05	.05	Driving Skills Affected
4	.15	.12	.11	.09	.08	.08	.07	.06	Possible Criminal Penalties
5	.19	.16	.13	.12	.11	.09	.09	.08	
6	.23	.19	.16	.14	.13	.11	.10	.09	Legally Intoxicated
7	.26	.22	.19	.16	.15	.13	.12	.11	
8	.30	.25	.21	.19	.17	.15	.14	.13	Criminal Penalties
9	.34	.28	.24	.21	.19	.17	.15	.14	
10	.38	.31	.27	.23	.21	.19	.17	.16	

Your body can get rid of one drink per hour.
Each 1½ oz. of 80 proof liquor, 12 oz. of beer or 5 oz. of table wine = 1 drink.

ALCOHOL IMPAIRMENT CHART

NEVER DRINK AND DRIVE

APPROXIMATE BLOOD ALCOHOL PERCENTAGE

Drinks	Body Weight in Pounds									
	90	100	120	140	160	180	200	220	240	
0	.00	.00	.00	.00	.00	.00	.00	.00	.00	ONLY SAFE DRIVING LIMIT
1	.05	.05	.04	.03	.03	.03	.02	.02	.02	Impairment Begins
2	.10	.09	.08	.07	.06	.05	.05	.04	.04	Driving Skills Affected
3	.15	.14	.11	.10	.09	.08	.07	.06	.06	Possible Criminal Penalties
4	.20	.18	.15	.13	.11	.10	.09	.08	.08	
5	.25	.23	.19	.16	.14	.13	.11	.10	.09	
6	.30	.27	.23	.19	.17	.15	.14	.12	.11	Legally Intoxicated
7	.35	.32	.27	.23	.20	.18	.16	.14	.13	
8	.40	.36	.30	.26	.23	.20	.18	.17	.15	Criminal Penalties
9	.45	.41	.34	.29	.26	.23	.20	.19	.17	
10	.51	.45	.38	.32	.28	.25	.23	.21	.19	

Your body can get rid of one drink per hour.
Each 1½ oz. of 80 proof liquor, 12 oz. of beer or 5 oz. of table wine = 1 drink.

COURTESY OF THE PENNSYLVANIA LIQUOR CONTROL BOARD

a breathalyzer. Depending on the circumstances, a more accurate reading of your BAC may be required. This is accomplished through a blood test.

Alcohol Poisoning

Alcohol poisoning can occur after you drink excessively. When your body absorbs too much alcohol in a short amount of time, it can affect your central nervous system by depressing nerves that slow your breathing, heart rate, and your gag reflex. Your gag reflex is what prevents choking. That is why it is paramount to turn someone on their side if they have passed out. Turning someone on their side can prevent him from choking.

One of the main reasons people vomit when they drink to excess is because alcohol irritates the stomach. If a person chokes when he vomits, he can easily die from asphyxiation. If a person is sleeping or passed out from alcohol, never assume he is out of danger. Alcohol that is in a person's stomach will still enter the blood stream even if he is unconscious.

SIGNS OF ALCOHOL POISONING

✓ Unresponsive, difficult to wake, or vomiting while sleeping.
✓ No response to pinching skin.
✓ Unable to rouse the person, almost coma-like.
✓ Seizures.
✓ Breathing is reduced or slowed.
✓ Irregular breathing.
✓ Hypothermia or low body temperature.

WHAT YOU CAN DO

✓ Any one of the signs above could be an indication of alcohol poisoning. You do not have to wait for *all* the signs to be present.
✓ Call for help immediately. This is a life-threatening situation.
✓ Carefully turn him on his side. By keeping him on his side, it will prevent him from choking if he vomits.

✓ Do not leave the person. Wait for EMS to arrive.
✓ If you are unsure what to do, call 911.

According to the NIAAA, even if the victim lives, an alcohol overdose can lead to irreversible brain damage. Rapid binge drinking, which often happens on a bet or a dare, is especially dangerous because the victim can ingest a fatal dose before becoming unconscious.

General "Partying" Safety: Know the Exits and Don't Panic

Without a doubt, spending time with friends and listening to a local band can make for a fun evening. Whether you're in a nightclub, a local restaurant, or a friend's apartment, it's very important that you have an awareness of the building you're in and your surroundings. This also holds true long after you have graduated from college.

On February 20, 2003, the heavy metal band Great White was playing at the Station nightclub in West Warwick, Rhode Island. The band enjoyed using pyrotechnics as part of their show. When the fireworks were ignited, the building caught fire, trapping many of the guests. With four possible exits from which to choose, most people stampeded the front door, the same door they entered earlier in the night. Unfortunately, with a crush of people charging at the same time, the hallway, and the front door entrance eventually became blocked.

Since the nightclub was built prior to 1976, it was not required to have a fire sprinkler system. Although heavy black smoke covered signs indicating the remaining three exits, they remained opened and passable. The fast-moving fire killed one hundred people, including many young adults, and injured more than two hundred.

A restaurant does not need a catastrophic fire to cause loss of life. On February 17, 2003, twenty-one people died and more than fifty were injured in a nightclub on the South Side of Chicago. It was not a fire that killed the young folks gathered; it was a stampede. In an attempt to break up a fight, a security officer apparently sprayed pepper spray, which started people scrambling for exits.

Reportedly with a lack of available exits on the second floor, patrons were forced to squeeze down a narrow stairway to the exit below. Many of the dead were trampled as they attempted to leave the building.

These incidents were preventable. Try this, the next time you're in a restaurant with friends or family, take a quick look around. Did the waitress seat you towards the rear of the dining room? Take note of the exits. Would you go back out the door from which you entered? If you're in a dingy, smoke-filled nightclub, or an apartment packed with students partying, do you think you could get out quickly if you had to? If you are in a nightclub, take a minute to walk around. Where would you go in case a fight broke out?

By simply being attentive to your environment, you will respond accordingly and make appropriate adjustments should a problem arise. When you're in any new setting, especially when alcohol is present, take a minute to familiarize yourself with the atmosphere. Listed below are a few suggestions that will assist you in being better prepared in the event an unforeseen incident occurs.

✓ Notice where all the exits are located.

✓ Never stay in a bar or restaurant that has any doors chained shut.

✓ Request a seat with an exit nearby.

✓ Are there battery-operated emergency lights above the exit signs?

✓ Are there windows in the room and are they accessible? Many buildings located in urban areas may have bars on the outside of the windows.

✓ If a crowd begins to become unruly, casually reposition yourself near an exit. Be proactive. Don't wait until a situation gets out of control—leave before a fight breaks out or chaos erupts.

✓ If something does happen, remain calm and look for the nearest exit. Do not automatically follow the crowd.

A Few Myths and Facts

As put forth by the National Institute on Alcohol Abuse and Alcoholism, NIAAA, these are a few of the myths that students have regarding alcohol.

Myth: I can drink and still be in control.

Fact: Drinking impairs your judgment, which increases the likelihood that you will do something you'll later regret, such as having unprotected sex, being involved in date rape, damaging property, or being victimized by others.

Myth: Drinking isn't all that dangerous.

Fact: One in three eighteen- to twenty-four-year-olds admitted to emergency rooms for serious injuries is intoxicated. Alcohol is also associated with homicides, suicides, and drownings.

Myth: I can sober up quickly if I have to.

Fact: It takes about three hours to eliminate the alcohol content of two drinks, depending on your weight. Nothing can speed up this process, not even coffee or cold showers.

Myth: It's okay for me to drink to keep up with my boyfriend.

Fact: Women process alcohol differently. No matter how much he drinks, if you drink the same amount as your boyfriend, you will be more intoxicated and more impaired.

Myth: I can manage to drive well enough after a few drinks.

Fact: About one-half of all fatal traffic crashes among eighteen- to twenty-four-year-olds involve alcohol. If you're under twenty-one, driving after drinking any alcohol is illegal, and you could lose your license. The risk of a fatal crash for drivers with positive BACs compared with other drivers (i.e., the relative risk) increases with increasing BAC, and the risks increase more steeply for drivers younger than age twenty-one than for older drivers.

Myth: I'd be better off if I learn to "hold my liquor."

Fact: If you have to drink increasingly larger amounts of alcohol to get a "buzz" or get "high," you are developing tolerance. Tolerance is actually a warning sign that you're developing more serious problems with alcohol.

Myth: Beer doesn't have as much alcohol as hard liquor.

Fact: A twelve-ounce bottle of beer has the same amount of alcohol as a standard shot of eighty-proof liquor (either straight or in a mixed drink) or five ounces of wine.

Take Responsibility the Extra Mile

So you're acting responsibly. You've made smart choices, which have led to safe results. Regrettably, not all students can say the same. If you're attentive throughout your college years, you will come across many students who are not as responsible as you are regarding alcohol. You may notice students who are extremely intoxicated or students who are in a dangerous situation. You might observe somebody who is passed out or too drunk to drive home.

Please, take a minute to assist these students if they are in need. The reality is some students will be unappreciative of your efforts, if they can remember at all. Their parents are sure to be grateful, but will never be informed. Becoming involved when you're not obligated proves a level of maturity well beyond basic responsibility. Your level of involvement may only require placing a phone call, but it could save someone's life. Here are a few suggestions to consider if you are able to offer assistance to someone who has been drinking.

- ✓ Be very cautious about putting yourself in danger.
- ✓ Never leave someone alone if they pass out. Turn him on his side. If you don't, and he vomits, he can easily choke on his vomit and die.
- ✓ Don't worry about getting the student in trouble.
- ✓ If you notice a student who's having difficulty walking, consider helping them home or notify campus security.
- ✓ If you are able, inquire as to the amount of alcohol the student had consumed.

✓ If a student is unresponsive, call 911 immediately. This is potentially life threatening.

✓ Don't assume that just because the person is back in his dorm that he will be fine. Inform an RA, or ask someone at the front desk to check on him. He may have alcohol poisoning.

✓ Don't give him a cold shower or coffee to sober him up. Only time will make him sober again.

✓ If you're unsure what to do, just call campus security. They'll help you and take control of the situation.

✓ LOOK OUT FOR EACH OTHER!

Do I Have a Problem?

Quite possibly, but don't punish yourself. Depending on your drinking habits in college, you may have to examine your history and ask, "Do I have a problem?" The term *alcoholic* can be scary, but don't get hung up on it. The definitive word is "problem." Having a problem with alcohol does not make you a bad person! Alcoholism is an illness.

Alcohol cuts across all spectrums of society; whether rich, poor, black, white, young, or old, alcohol does not discriminate. It has no boundaries. The good news is you are not alone. Literally, millions of people have the same problem. Right now, in the town where you are reading this book, I would venture to say there are multiple locations for Alcoholics Anonymous meetings. The Bowles Center for Alcohol Studies put together the following twenty questions for students, to assist you in determining whether you might have a problem with alcohol.

1. Do you lose time from classes due to drinking?
2. Do you drink because you are uncomfortable in social situations?
3. Do you drink to build up your self confidence?
4. Is drinking affecting your relationship with friends?
5. Do you drink alone?
6. Do you drink to escape from studies or home worries?
7. Do you feel guilty or depressed after drinking?

8. Does it bother you if someone says that maybe you drink too much?
9. Do you have to take a drink when you go out on a date?
10. Do you get along better with other people when you drink?
11. Do you get into financial troubles over buying liquor?
12. Do you feel more important when you drink?
13. Have you lost friends since you started drinking?
14. Do you drink more than most of your friends?
15. Have you started hanging around with a crowd that drinks more than your old friends?
16. Do you drink until you just couldn't drink anymore?
17. Have you ever had a complete loss of memory from drinking?
18. Have you ever been to a hospital or been arrested due to drunken behavior?
19. Do you turn off any studies of lectures about drinking?
20. Do you think you have a problem with alcohol?

If you answered yes to some of these questions, you have some of the symptoms that indicate a problem with alcohol. Remember, there's no reason to deny that you have a health problem. If you think you do have a problem, the most important thing is to do something about it!

No one is recommending that you make a public proclamation that you drink more than you should. I am simply suggesting that making a decision to at least investigate what options are available might be a course of action to consider. Requesting help for a possible drinking problem may be one of the smartest choices you'll ever make. A great place to start is logging onto www.alcoholics-anonymous.org.

Drugs on Campus

I'm sorry to say there are drugs on almost every campus, but I suspect you already knew that. In the beginning of this chapter, I spoke about the barrage of decisions you'll make on a daily basis. Some decisions are obviously more significant than others. Students participate in excessive drinking because of the perceived social acceptability and their naiveté regarding the immense dangers. Nevertheless, consuming alcohol is a legal activity when you turn twenty-one—doing drugs is illegal at any age.

You would think that among marijuana, cocaine, LSD, crack, heroin, crystal-meth, ecstasy, and a host of other illicit narcotics, the selection for drugs users would be quite adequate. However, as in any capitalist society, new ideas are always on the horizon, and that includes enterprising drug addicts. *Pharming* is all the rage on college campuses. No, I'm not talking about a guy with twenty acres and a John Deere tractor. I'm speaking about students who use and deal in prescription drugs as a mechanism to get high.

According to a report from Joseph A. Califano, chairman of the National Center on Addiction and Substance Abuse, at Columbia University, and author of the book, *High Society*, from 1993 to 2005, the proportion of students who abuse prescription painkillers like Percocet, Vicodin, and Oxycontin shot up 343 percent to 240,000 students. Stimulants like Ritalin and Adderall, increased 93 percent to 225,000 students. Tranquilizers like Xanax and Valium rose 450 percent to 171,000, and sedatives like Nembutal and Seconal, 225 percent to 101,000 students.

I sincerely doubt pharming will overtake the Colombian drug cartel, but it will certainly leave an indelible mark on society if it continues at its current growth rate. "Accepting as inevitable this college culture of alcohol and other drug abuse threatens not only the present well being of millions of college students, but also the future capacity of our nation to maintain its leadership in the fiercely competitive global economy," said Joseph Califano.

I suspect to a large degree that the genesis of escalating drug use on college campuses begins at home. However, with multiple agencies reporting an increase in drug use in America's high schools and colleges, the time to reevaluate our country's anti-drug programs is now! Making a conscientious choice to partake in illicit drugs is akin to playing Russian Roulette with the rest of your life. The consequences of such destructive behavior can jeopardize your entire future.

I'm going to assume most of you have either tried drugs, have been asked to participate in doing drugs, or know someone who currently uses drugs. Look, if you're being honest, you know as well as I do that there is not one good thing that comes from taking drugs, not one! Can you say for certain how your body will react to a foreign substance entering it? Perhaps you'll get a buzz the first time you get high. Do you know how your body will react the second time? How about the third time? Are you willing to bet your life on it?

✓ Are you willing to participate in an illegal activity all in the name of being cool?

✓ Are you willing to purposefully damage your body?

✓ Are you willing to risk arrest, a police record, and a criminal background?

✓ Are you willing to risk future employment prospects?

✓ Are you willing to risk the failure of a company drug test?

✓ Are you willing to risk the vetting process a corporation may put you through?

✓ Are you willing to risk the shame and embarrassment to your family?

✓ Are you willing to risk a potential lifelong addiction?

✓ Are you willing to risk a rapid decline in your financial future?

✓ Are you willing to risk long-term health problems?

✓ Are you willing to risk death for a twenty-minute buzz?

The decision is yours—make the smart choice!

5

It's Spring Break!

When Jennifer met her roommate, Lisa, for the first time at freshman orientation, she was a little concerned. Lisa came from a bigger town and appeared more forward than Jennifer. Lisa liked to have fun, a lot of fun. But despite Lisa's apparent party reputation, she was great. Lisa's consideration was evident when they visited their dorm room together for the first time. She asked Jennifer which bed she'd like, which desk, and which bookcase. When their laundry basket was full the first week of school, Lisa not only did Jennifer's laundry, but also folded it and put it away. Could a roommate ask for anything more?

After their freshman year there would be no doubt Lisa and Jennifer would room together their sophomore year. The girls chatted all summer and were excited to reunite in August to begin their second year of college. Although they lived in a coed dorm, the girls did not give the guys much thought on move-in weekend; they were too engrossed in catching up. As the beginning weeks of the fall semester rolled on, the girls fell into their class schedule during the week and partying routine during the weekend.

Jennifer quickly learned that she really could not keep up with Lisa when they partied together. Many weekends during their freshman year, Jennifer sat up with Lisa after a night of beer-pong. Helping Lisa to the bathroom and getting her back in bed became customary on the weekends. Although

Lisa was crowned beer-pong champion two months in a row, there were actually girls in the dorm who drank much more and did worse things.

Lisa enjoyed partying. She took pleasure in meeting people and making new friends. However, in the course of doing so, she had a tendency to go overboard. Her aggressiveness not withstanding, Lisa really brought the girls in the dorm together, especially the girls on the third floor. When October rolled around, Lisa noticed a travel company on campus handing out flyers for next year's Spring Break. She brought twenty flyers back to the dorm and passed them out each with a handwritten note, "This is us! Meeting in the third floor lounge this Thursday . . . 8 p.m."

The lounge was packed. It was standing room only. Lisa being Lisa was front and center calling the meeting to order. Although many in attendance knew they were unable to attend Spring Break, the girls were close friends and really enjoyed the preliminary planning meeting. After five subsequent meetings, it was set. Twelve girls from the third floor, including Lisa and Jennifer, were flying to south Florida next March. They booked three rooms with four girls per room.

With Christmas break over and only days away from departing, the anticipation of Spring Break in Florida was almost too much to bear for the girls from the third floor. Many nights were spent researching every aspect of the trip. The hotel amenities, the hot spots, and the nightclubs were reviewed for months before the trip. Yes, they anticipated the guys, too. Although everyone going on this trip was under the legal drinking age of twenty-one, the girls knew of every beer bash and booze cruise within twenty miles. The question wasn't how to get in—it was, "Which drinking fest do we attend?"

At last they were in Florida, having a great time, and for the most part, behaving well. After breakfast they would scope out a spot on the beach and be set up by 10 a.m. The guys would come around right on cue. Similar to a fisherman throwing a bucket of chum in the water to attract the fish, once the girls hit the beach wearing their bikinis, the guys began circling like sharks around a shipwreck.

Jennifer and Lisa enjoyed the attention. So did the other girls. By lunchtime, the guys would usually inform the girls of the hot-spot beer bashes.

Knowing the girls had to wear wristbands indicating they were not twenty-one, the guys reassured them they would feed them beers. It was day four of the trip, and this group of guys seemed very nice. They were from a college in the Midwest and had spent the past two days together hanging out on the beach and dancing at the nightclubs. The guys were protective of the girls and appeared to be gentlemen.

As day six approached, the girls from the third floor spent most of their time with their new friends. Karen, one of the girls in the group, didn't come home the previous night but insisted that nothing happened when she returned. "Yeah right," Lisa said. "What happened? The last time we saw you, you were dancing with Brian, where'd you guys go?" "We went back to his hotel to hang out for a while, and we both fell asleep on the couch. Honestly, we were just lying on his couch and the next thing you knew we were sleeping. He really is very nice," Karen said.

Jennifer and Lisa also really liked their new Spring Break buddies and wanted to spend some time alone with them before they went back home. Although the girls decided earlier in the week that it would be okay if a guy slept over, none of the girls from the third floor had invited their new guy friends to stay the night.

About 3 a.m. Saturday morning, the morning they flew home, everyone was in bed when Jennifer stumbled in the door. She walked over to the couch, sat down, curled up her legs, and buried her head in her lap. Not sure what was going on, and still somewhat awake, Lisa turned on the light.

Jennifer was on the couch sobbing and shaking. Her shirt was ripped, and she had dirt and sand all over her. As she lifted her head, Lisa yelled, "Holy shit, Jennifer, what happened?" Jennifer's face was bloody. Her lip and nose were slightly bleeding and her left eye was black and blue. Her long brown hair was knotted and disheveled. Lisa yelled to Karen, "Call the police!"

Jennifer immediately snapped, "Don't call the police. I'll be fine. Just give me a couple minutes." It was obvious her friend was badly assaulted, but Lisa feared the worst. In a calming voice, Lisa said, "Jenn, it's just us, tell me what happened." As Jennifer began to recount the evening, Karen came from the bathroom with wet towels to clean the dirt off her friend.

"When we left the bar, Dave suggested we go for a walk on the beach. I thought it was a nice idea. We walked back to the hotel pool and grabbed a few towels. There were a bunch of people on the beach, so we just walked further down, away from everyone. I still don't get it. We were lying on the towels and started fooling around. I didn't think anything of it. The next thing I know I'm half undressed, and he kept saying, 'Come on, it's been a great week.' It's like I wanted to, but I didn't, you know? The more I kept saying 'no,' the rougher he got. Next thing I know, his forearm is across my face, and my head is pinned in the sand. God, he was so strong, I couldn't move him. Every time my head moved, he buried his arm harder in my face. I couldn't even talk. I'll be okay. I handled it. Promise you won't say a word to anyone. I'll just tell my parents I fell."

Lisa and Karen kept the promise their friend asked of them. Two months after Spring Break, Jennifer entered counseling at school. Upon the counselor's recommendation, Jennifer contacted the police in Florida and filed a rape report. The police took the report and told her they would look into it. Jennifer only knew the boy's name, Dave, and the hotel where he had stayed. She told the police he was from the Midwest, but as the police know all too well, many of the things he told her may not be true.

Each year, over a million college students flock to the warm Florida and Mexican sun for what is supposed to be a respite from their studies. Europe and the Caribbean are also becoming hot spots for the annual college vacation. But the innocence of relaxing on the beach with friends has been taken over by high-risk behavior, MTV's Spring Break, Girls Gone Wild, and the Las Vegas adage of "What happens on Spring Break stays at Spring Break."

Spring Break requires special preparation. Spring Break vacations are not the annual family trip to the beach. It's fast moving with a lot of action. If you're not properly informed and armed with the knowledge to keep yourself safe, you could quickly find yourself in trouble. Every year students are robbed, raped, put in jail, and injured in accidents, spending nights in emergency rooms. Some are killed.

Dr. Frederick Epstein, chair of emergency medicine at Bay Medical Center, in Panama City, Florida, as well as the Bay County Emergency Medical Services, told the *American Medical News* magazine when speaking of Spring Break, "We brace emotionally and I'm very happy when they're all gone. I've grown weary after some years of finding myself having to make a long-distance phone call to an unwitting parent who doesn't even realize that their son or daughter is in Panama City. It's always difficult to preside over the pronouncement of death of anybody, but it's particularly difficult when I have to call and wake someone up in the middle of the night to tell them that their son or daughter has expired down here. They're strangers and I can't even look them in the face."

Although the crimes and accidents that occur on Spring Break are not physically on college campuses, Spring Break is very much an extension of college life. Because so little has been written about the hazards of Spring Break, this topic could be considered somewhat controversial. Controversy notwithstanding, Spring Break is a real problem for many unsuspecting students.

The Spring Break chapter will offer suggestions to those of you who are leaving for their Spring Break destination. Tips are also offered for students who are traveling to Mexico and other foreign countries.

Booking the Trips

Has the following conversation ever taken place in your home?

"Mom, I think we're all going to go to Cancun this year."

"Andrea, why do you want to go to Cancun?"

"Well, it's cheaper. And besides, that's where everyone is going this year."

"I'd prefer you to stay in this country."

"But Mom, everyone in my dorm is going. They've already booked the trip. It's at a great resort. I'll pay for it."

"Fine, if that's where you want to go. But there better not be a lot of drinking! I'm not kidding, Andrea. You guys better be good!"

"Mom, we'll be fine!"

Why do students book trips with certain tour companies? Are travel agencies promoting dangerous drinking and sex to lure students? Do they market countries where the drinking age is only eighteen? Are some tour promoters emphasizing countries where it's legal to smoke marijuana? You be the judge, but here are the facts.

According to an American Medical Association survey, 91 percent of parents say it's time to stop Spring Break marketing and promotional practices that promote dangerous drinking. Dr. J. Edward Hill, AMA chair-elect says, "The tourism and alcohol industries promote heavy drinking and sex, creating an environment that can lead to rape, fatal injuries, and death by alcohol poisoning. We agree with parents that we must put an end to these promotions that target students."

The American Medical Association's, "A Matter of Degree" poll indicated the following:

- ✔ 56 percent of parents were completely unaware that tour companies market Spring Break destinations directly to college students, emphasizing heavy drinking and sex.
- ✔ 91 percent of 500 parents surveyed say it's time to stop Spring Break marketing and promotional practices that promote dangerous drinking.
- ✔ More than 80 percent of parents said they were concerned about college students drinking alcohol during Spring Break.
- ✔ 71 percent of parents were concerned about students having unprotected sex.
- ✔ 70 percent of parents were concerned about student driving while intoxicated or with a drunken driver.
- ✔ 68 percent of parents were concerned about female students being raped.
- ✔ 88 percent of parents said they think that Spring Break is primarily a problem of underage drinking because many college students are younger than the legal drinking age of twenty-one.
- ✔ 61 percent of parents believe that underage students are more likely to drink than twenty-one-year-olds.

In July, 2007, the website www.studentspringbreak.com talked about booking a trip to Cancun: "Benefits of going to Cancun are many, yes, but most students just care about the abundance of alcohol, alcohol and wait, you guessed it, more alcohol. Your yearly intake of alcoholic consumption could happen in one small week in Cancun, Mexico, on Spring Break."

The website continues to coach the student should their parent begin to question their trip. It states, "For those of you worried about what your parents might say, tell them it's an 'educational trip.' You are working to graduate college with a minor in heavy drinking. And best of all Mom, I don't have to worry about drinking the water and getting sick, because I will only be drinking beer. For all of the novice drinkers out there, remember this fail-proof saying to avoid near catastrophe while you're in Cancun: Beer before liquor makes you sicker, liquor before beer you're in the clear."

Consider this ad for a student trip to Amsterdam: the lead paragraph on www.studentspringbreak.com states: "Amster – dam there is a lot of pot there. Who hasn't heard that Amsterdam is a pot-smoker's paradise? The myth is true. The socialist government extends to the people of Holland and their liberal lifestyle. Not only that, but Amsterdam is home to dykes, bikes, and Anne Frank. Not all in that order of course." Another tour company offers a "sign-up bonus of 20-50 hours of free drinks at most of our international locations."

Whether or not someone considers these travel and tour companies reckless, many students travel on these kinds of trips. However, other options do exist for Spring Break. Ski trips and service-oriented vacations such as building houses in hurricane-ravaged areas are becoming popular.

Regardless of the trip you've scheduled, precautions must be taken. Preparation before you leave for any location is absolutely essential. Find out the laws of the town or the laws of the country you will be visiting. Prior to leaving, make sure your medical insurance is accepted in the town you're visiting. Have an emergency or "what if" plan. Also, know your surroundings at all times. Even if you are unsure, act like you know what you're doing.

Prior to Leaving on Spring Break

It's understandable that you're excited to leave on break. Whether you're traveling to some exotic destination or spending time at home bugging your younger brother, it's prudent not to overlook basic precautions while you're away.

- ✓ Make sure you book your trip with a reputable travel agent. Ask to see brochures of the hotel.
- ✓ Know exactly what's included in your package.
- ✓ Unplug appliances, stereos, and other electronic devices prior to leaving.
- ✓ Make sure all windows and doors are locked.
- ✓ Take all your garbage out before you leave, or you may have an interesting aroma when you return.
- ✓ Make sure you pack all medications and other personal necessities.
- ✓ It's a good idea to purchase an inexpensive timer for the lights or a lamp. Stagger the time when the lights turn on and off. Make sure you don't have any fabric near or covering a lamp or light fixture that's set on an automatic timer.
- ✓ Confirm your hotel reservations before you leave town.
- ✓ Keep an eye on your valuables at all times. Try not to carry large sums of cash. Traveler's checks are accepted in almost every Spring Break location.

Driving to Spring Break

Depending where you live, driving to your Spring Break destination is not a bad alternative. In many cases it's recommended. However, like anything else, it comes with its own set of considerations. The following list of suggestions will help you prepare for your road trip.

- ✓ Make sure your vehicle is in good working order prior to leaving. Better yet, have a mechanic check its condition.
- ✓ Have your car tuned up and tires checked.

✓ Have you ever changed a flat tire? If not, jack up your vehicle in your driveway and practice removing the tire.

✓ Plan your trip, and map it out before you leave.

✓ Make sure you understand how to read a map.

✓ Use caution when taking back roads. Drive on interstates as much as possible.

✓ Don't pick up any hitchhikers or stop to help someone who is flagging you down. Call the police on your cell phone, and give them the location of the person in need.

✓ Have hotels booked prior to departing or you just may find yourself sleeping in the car.

✓ Check in with your parents or a friend along the way.

✓ Get sufficient rest before a long driving stretch.

✓ If you find yourself getting sleepy, pull over immediately. Driving when fatigued is similar to driving drunk.

✓ Don't drive all night. If you do pull over to sleep, make sure the car is in a very well-lit area, and keep it locked while you're sleeping.

✓ If your car does breakdown, stay in the car and call the police. If people stop and offer assistance, don't get out of the car. Ask them to call police for you if you don't have a cell phone available.

✓ Give parents or a friend your driving itinerary.

✓ Respect all speed limits and local traffic laws.

✓ Once at your Spring Break destination, exercise extreme caution when driving or cruising around town.

✓ You've heard it a million times before, but don't drink and drive. Save the partying until you arrive.

Traveling in the United States

Although Cancun and other countries are becoming popular Spring Break destinations, beach resorts in the United States are still the first choice for college students. No matter what your destination is, don't assume all laws and ordinances are the same. One law is universal, however. The legal drinking age in all fifty states is twenty-one. If you're caught drinking underage, you will be cited and possibly arrested. If you're caught using fake ID, criminal penalties may also be imposed.

While businesses welcome the revenue Spring Break generates—it's important to remember that the town you're visiting is *home* to thousands of people. Their businesses, churches, children, and schools are the epicenter of their lives, and as such, Spring Break can be disruptive to the locals.

Students tend to think that they're anonymous when they're away from college, away from home, and away from family. As a result, they do things on Spring Break that they would never consider doing at home or even at college. Consequently, being drunk and disorderly is commonplace. Fortunately, police and security personnel will respond swiftly. Please, be respectful when visiting these towns.

Many males think they're invulnerable; they're not. No matter where you're going, always travel with someone, or better yet, take a third person. This is especially true for the girls. When you're walking on the beach or to the bars at night, make sure you have others with you and carry identification.

Use caution when milling about the streets or attending parties where large numbers of people are gathered. You can be walking along minding your own business, and problems can arise very quickly. Innocently bumping into someone can be perceived as looking for trouble. Cutting in line, especially a beer line, could result in an all-out brawl. Just glancing at someone's date or accidentally spilling a drink on someone is reason for a fight. Certain guys get beer muscles, and after a few drinks they can rationalize everything they do. What starts as pushing and shoving could end up with you being escorted from the nightclub, or worse, arrested.

With cameras everywhere, anonymity isn't what it used to be; so think before you make a fool of yourself. Something you do on Spring Break may just come back and haunt you years from now. This wasn't much of a concern ten years ago. But technology has changed exponentially. Cell phone cameras, digital cameras, and camcorders are everywhere. Oh, did I mention cell phone cameras? When you see a cell phone, think "camera." I promise you this; you are not nearly as anonymous as you think you are. If your picture was taken, there is a very good chance it will end up on the Internet.

✎ Hot Tip:
If someone takes your picture and puts it on the Internet, you will have a better chance of the Pope coming for Easter dinner than having your photo removed.

As you're walking the resort streets, you will experience a host of sights unlike any other. Due to the very large crowds, many beach towns will have police and medics on motorcycles and bicycles to enable them to traverse the crowded roads. I know *you* wouldn't think of participating, but you will see girls "flashing" or exposing themselves for beads. This has become very popular. Depending on the town, you *will* be arrested, and so will the people egging you on.

Students on Spring Break are a criminal's candy store. Every week, the criminals are there, waiting for the shelves to be restocked with new treats . . . you. The crooks are informed. They know when you arrive you'll have ample cash in your pocket. They'll watch and wait, being very patient. They notice when you put your belongings on the beach. They observe the wad of bills in your pocket when you buy a few beers. Just when you and your friends are into the second set of beer volleyball, they will disappear with your valuables.

No matter where you go for Spring Break, crimes and accidents will not be far behind. Exercising restraint and implementing common sense precautions will lessen the likelihood of you becoming a crime or an accident statistic.

- ✓ Do not drive with anyone who has been dinking!
- ✓ Know the local and state laws where you will be staying.
- ✓ Do not trust anyone you meet! Trust must be earned. People could

be giving you a bogus name, town, or even a hotel where they are staying.

✓ Have a plan before you go out.

✓ Make sure your family knows exactly where you'll be on Spring Break. Give them a complete itinerary of flight schedules, hotels, and room numbers when you check in.

✓ Make sure your family knows with whom you will be traveling and their family's information.

✓ Check in daily with your family.

✓ Always walk in well-lit areas.

✓ When walking day or night, do so with authority. Follow your instincts, and be aware of the people around you.

✓ Always be aware of your surroundings, whether on the beach, in the water, or at the bars.

✓ Even if you *think* you know this person you met a few days ago, use extreme caution. More females are sexually assaulted by acquaintances than by strangers.

✓ Keep all cash and valuables out of sight.

✓ Bring traveler's checks and minimal cash.

✓ Do not bring all of your credit cards or bank cards.

✓ When at the beach or clubs, keep your keys and cash hidden.

✓ Be careful not to openly display your cash when paying for things. It can also be a good idea to put cash in different pockets.

✓ LOOK OUT FOR EACH OTHER!

Mexico and Other International Trips

The U.S. Department of State's Spring Break website says, "Over 100,000 American teenagers and young adults travel to resort areas throughout Mexico over Spring Break each year. While the vast majority enjoys their vacation without incident, several may die, hundreds will be arrested, and still more will make mistakes that could affect them for the rest of their lives. Using some common sense will help travelers avoid these unpleasant and dangerous situations."

The State Department's caveat is certainly not encouraging for travel to Mexico. While Mexico has very specific warnings listed on the State Department's website, other countries can be equally dangerous. Parts of Jamaica, Haiti, and South America are known for their drug trafficking and gang violence. It's imperative to research the country you're contemplating visiting. A great place to start is the U.S. Department of State's travel website, www.travel.state.gov. The website features detailed information on passports, visas, and consular programs, as well as provides in-depth international travel advice.

It's extremely important to understand the laws of the country you're visiting. While underage drinking, drug use, disorderly conduct, and fighting are minor infractions in the United States, they may be considered major criminal offenses in foreign countries. If you're arrested in Mexico, it's not uncommon to remain there for up to a year before you would have a hearing. Your parents may send thousands of dollars for your release from prison only to be informed, "Nunca recibimos su dinero"—translated, we never received your money. The Mexican criminal justice system is not for the faint of heart. Jails in Mexico and other third world countries can make our prison system look like a Hilton Hotel.

Other considerations when traveling abroad include the service sector and the abilities of underdeveloped countries to respond to your needs and requests. Hospital services, police departments, fire departments, building codes, restaurant cleanliness, nightclub safety measures like sprinkler systems and EMS services may be significantly diminished or nonexistent. Safety precautions may be in place in large resorts within a compound, but travel outside the resort area increases substantially your chances of becoming a victim of a crime or an accident.

The recent unsettling news about Mexico is nothing new. In January, 2003, *USA Today* reported—according to the U.S. Consulate in Mexico, during the eight-week break period in 2002,—"U.S. students accounted for two deaths, 360 arrests, four injuries that required medical evacuations out of the area, one rape, 495 reports of lost or stolen property, and 504 'general welfare inquiries'—usually from parents back in the USA who were worried about a students' whereabouts."

✎ Hot Tip:

Without question, the number one rule for traveling abroad is to log on to this website, www.travel.state.gov, and research your overseas destination. Here, you'll find up-to-date, official travel warnings about various countries, safety and health information, and general guidance for international travel.

Former top State Department officer in Merida, Mexico, Consul Glen Keiser, told *USA Today*, "That's what ties all of our cases together, excessive drinking. Booze, sex and acting like idiots. The hardest thing I have to do is call a parent in the United States and tell them their son or daughter has died." Keiser went on to say, "Kids get down here and they think the rules are off, well, they are wrong."

Before departing for any international trip, contact your health insurance provider and make sure your medical insurance is accepted in your destination country. There is a very good chance your insurance will *not* be accepted. If it is not accepted, you are strongly urged to purchase travel insurance, or a short-term policy designed to cover travel-related emergencies. It's imperative that your coverage includes medical evacuation to the United States. The State Department says that a medical evacuation can cost more than $50,000.

Travel insurance policies can be customized according to your trip and needs. They cover a myriad of options and services from lost luggage and missed cruise departures to hospital visits and emergency medical flights home. Many policy premiums are based on your age, cost of trip, and length overseas. Travel insurance could cost as much as two hundred dollars. However, not being covered in a medical emergency in a distant country could cost a staggering amount of money.

Here are additional precautions to consider before traveling to a foreign destination.

- ✓ Before you leave on break, find the numbers of the U.S. Consulate specific to your country and any other U.S. official offices. Call the State Department before you leave and ask for the numbers directly if you cannot locate them.
- ✓ Apply for your passport well in advance of your trip. Recent changes to the law have made a passport necessary for travel to Mexico, Canada, and parts of the Caribbean (areas that previously did not require a passport). These changes have caused many delays in processing. Apply as soon as possible. Check to see if your passport needs to be renewed. Renew your passport if it's close to the expiration date. You may encounter problems if traveling too close to your passport's expiration date—renew your passport at least six to eight months before the expiration date.
- ✓ Familiarize yourself with the laws of the country you'll be visiting. The U.S. Department of State lists specific details for most countries on their website.
- ✓ Notify your doctor and tell him the country you will be traveling to and ask if there are any medical precautions you must take.
- ✓ Purchase plenty of "international" calling cards. Contact the hotel or resort prior to departing and find out acceptable phone companies and cards. This is crucial. Calling the United States even from the Caribbean can be very difficult at times.
- ✓ Make sure you have diarrhea medication.
- ✓ Carry small bills.
- ✓ Make sure you carry your driver's license or passport wherever you go.
- ✓ Most hotels have their own water-filtration system; however the water and ice may still be contaminated.
- ✓ Make sure food is served hot.
- ✓ Avoid salads and fruit.

✓ Never, ever take a package from anyone. You may be offered cash or free trips to carry a small package in your suitcase. Most of these packages contain drugs. If caught, you will be subject to the country's drug laws.

Hotel Safety

Most hotels are relatively safe buildings, even in foreign countries. Major hotel chains and resorts have strict building codes. However, small independent stand-alone motels may not require stringent code enforcement overseas. Regardless of where you're staying, the responsibility for your safety will fall squarely on you.

Fires and natural disasters can and do strike hotels. Remember the videos of the tsunami hitting the Sri Lanka resort in December 2004? Over the years, however, many problems in hotels are due to overzealous students carrying their fun a bit too far.

✓ Try to research your hotel and double-check your reservations prior to leaving on break.

✓ Know exactly where all the exits are located on your floor.

✓ Know what's outside your window or balcony.

✓ Don't leave your door unlocked or open if you go down the hall.

✓ Don't horseplay on or near the balconies.

✓ Never try to jump into the pool from the balcony. Yes, people have tried, and they have died.

✓ Don't try to climb from balcony to balcony for any reason.

✓ Never sit on the railings of balconies.

✓ Don't unlock or tamper with the balcony doors if they're locked. Many hotels lock the balconies for Spring Break. If they're unlocked, you will be instantly evicted from the hotel and arrested in many cases.

✓ Don't overcrowd the elevators.

✓ Keep your door locked at all times.

✓ Make sure you know who is at the door when someone knocks. If the door doesn't have a peephole, ask who it is before answering.

Hitting the Beach

I realize you didn't spend your time and money traveling to a beach resort to hang out in the hotel. You're looking to spend time in the sun and splash around in the blue water. The sun in tropical locations is extremely powerful, so it's important to use a lot of common sense when outside during the day.

✓ Limit the amount of sunlight you receive between 10 a.m. and 4 p.m.
✓ Continually apply sunscreen with an SPF of at least 15. Reapply after swimming.
✓ Wear a hat. Purchase a hat at the resort if you have to, but wear one.
✓ Make sure your sunglasses have UV (ultraviolet) protection.
✓ Don't fall asleep in the sun.
✓ Drink plenty of water when at the beach, even if you're not thirsty.

Additionally, limit the amount of valuables and cash you take to the beach. (In fact, don't travel with valuables such as jewelry or high-priced electronics period). If you go for a swim, make sure someone from your group stays behind to keep an eye on your belongings. Before you venture out into the high seas, here are a few precautions to consider:

✓ Swim near a lifeguard.
✓ Don't swim alone.
✓ Let someone know you're going in the water.
✓ Never swim at night.
✓ Never swim after you've been drinking.
✓ Don't swim near piers, rocks, jetties, or pilings.
✓ If you're stung by a jellyfish, notify the lifeguard. Vinegar or meat tenderizer will reduce the pain.

FLAGS

Lifeguards on many beaches use a colored-flag system to inform swimmers of water conditions. Depending on where you're located, the flags may differ in color. It's very important to familiarize yourself with the beach flags on your beach. It would not make for a good day if you are unknowingly swimming in excessively high levels of bacteria, just because you were not aware of the flag warning. A few universal colors are listed below.

Red Flags: Stay out of the water. Strong undertow, rip currents, or elevated bacteria levels.

Yellow Flags: Use caution in the water. Undertow, rip currents, or bacteria are possible.

Blue Flags: Calm water.

Purple Flags: Dangerous marine life is present.

Rip Currents

No question—rip currents are a cause for concern. According to the United States Lifesaving Association (USLA), more than 100 people die in rip currents in the United States each year. Rips are powerful, but they are absolutely survivable!

Without getting too technical, a rip current is a channeled current of water that flows away from shore. They can occur at any beach with breaking waves, but they will not suck you under like an undertow. If you don't panic, you can ride a rip current until it stops.

So what to do? Yes, you will feel as though you are getting "pulled" out to sea. Don't worry; no one has ever taken a rip current to Europe. Also, rip currents are not that wide, sometimes only twenty to thirty feet across. The National Oceanic and Atmospheric Administration (NOAA) has a great description of a rip current and the appropriate course of action if caught in one (visit www.noaa.gov, and type in "rip current"). NOAA states, "Think of it like a treadmill that cannot be turned off, which you need to step to the side of."

✓ Relax! Don't panic.
✓ Tread water or lay on your back.
✓ Scream for help, and wave your hands.

✓ Never try to swim against the current. It *will* wear you out.
✓ Even though you're moving away from shore, swim sideways following the shoreline. You may not have to swim very far. Eventually, the pulling sensation will stop.
✓ Once out of the rip current, swim at an angle towards shore, but away from the current.

Time to Party

The excessive amount of alcohol available to Spring Break students is unimaginable, and many times reckless. Combining the inexperience of a student with an endless supply of alcohol is not only dangerous but potentially lethal. All-you-can-drink specials, beer-soaked parties, and alcohol-themed beach bashes are taken to the extreme on a daily basis during the weeks of Spring Break.

Amongst the craziness of the nightclubs and parties, it's easy to get caught up in the action and let your guard down. Pay attention to who's pouring the drinks. Make sure they're coming from the bartender, not a person you just met. Watch your friends. If they begin to act strangely or do things out of the ordinary, even for their personality, don't leave them. Don't make it easier for someone to sexually assault you by drinking over your limit. Also, many towns have open-container laws that prohibit driving or even walking on the sidewalk with an open beer. There's a very good chance you'll be cited if caught with an open beer or mixed drink of any kind.

The University of Wisconsin conducted a study that found 75 percent of college males and 43.6 percent of females reported being intoxicated on a daily basis during Spring Break. Nearly half of the males and more than 40 percent of the females also reported being drunk to the point of vomiting or passing out at least once during the break. According to the same study, only a few students who had sex during Spring Break used condoms, even if condoms were available. And among women, those with a higher alcohol consumption were more likely to have been the victim of a sexual assault.

Alcohol-soaked trips and students drinking to excess are nothing new. In May, 1998, the *Journal of American College of Health* reported, "During

Spring Break, the average male reported drinking 18 drinks per day and the average woman reported 10 drinks per day. More than half of all men and more than 40 percent of all women drank until they became sick or passed out at least once."

Look, there's no way I can tell you to just have a beer or two and call it quits. It's not reality, and I know that. However, it's not unreasonable for anyone to expect that you take a more direct role in your personal safety by not putting yourself in a compromising position in the first place. By following basic guidelines you significantly reduce your exposure and diminish the likelihood of becoming a statistic.

✓ Don't drive with anyone who has been drinking!

✓ Pace yourself! It's a long week.

✓ Plan, plan, plan before you go out. Plan the number of drinks you will consume and plan on how to say no once you reach your drink limit.

✓ Make sure you eat well before you drink, and snack on food while you're drinking.

✓ Keep track of how many drinks you've had throughout the day.

✓ When you're with your group of friends, take turns *not* drinking for one day. This will enable you to keep an eye on each other.

✓ Never leave a party or bar with someone you don't know, and never let your friends go off with someone they've just met.

✓ If you're in a bar or club, make sure you know exactly where *all* of the exits are located. If the bar is crowded, try to sit as close to an exit as possible. Bar fights are not uncommon, and if they occur, you want to leave as soon as possible. In the event of a fire, you will need to be prepared by knowing all the exits.

✓ If your friends have too much to drink, don't leave them alone.

✓ If you've had too much to drink, tell a friend to stay with you.

✓ If your friend is drunk and passes out, turn him on his side and never leave him alone. If you don't turn him on his side, and he vomits, he could easily choke. If you're unsure what to do, call 911.

✓ Don't accept a drink from a stranger or someone you've just met.

✓ Try to watch the bartender make your drink.

✓ Never set down your drink, even for a second. Whether you're drinking soda or alcohol, don't walk away from your drink. Take it with you to the restroom if you must. Never accept a drink from a stranger. Date-rape drugs are easily slipped in drinks, especially in foreign countries.

✓ Use caution walking back to the hotel from the clubs. There's a very good chance that some people driving are drunk. Pay attention to where you are walking, and stay on the sidewalks as much as possible.

✓ LOOK OUT FOR EACH OTHER!

Alcohol Poisoning

Drinking excessive alcohol can quickly turn into alcohol poisoning. When you're drinking and your body absorbs too much alcohol in a short amount of time, it can affect your central nervous system by depressing nerves that slow your breathing, heart rate, and your gag reflex. If you're observant during Spring Break, it's likely you'll see someone who has alcohol poisoning. This is life threatening. Help them if you can!

SIGNS OF ALCOHOL POISONING

✓ Unresponsive, difficult to wake, or vomiting while sleeping

✓ No response to pinching skin

✓ Unable to rouse the person, almost coma-like

✓ Seizures

✓ Breathing is reduced or slowed

✓ Irregular breathing

✓ Hypothermia or low body temperature

WHAT YOU CAN DO

✓ Any one of the signs above could be an indication of alcohol poisoning. You don't have to wait for *all* the signs to be present.

✓ Call for help immediately. This is a life-threatening situation.
✓ Carefully turn him on his side. By keeping him on his side, it will prevent him from choking if he vomits.
✓ Don't leave the person. Wait for EMS to arrive.
✓ If you're unsure what to do, call 911.

Alternative Spring Break

Perhaps you're at a point in your life where booze cruises, wet T-shirt contests, and vomiting in the street are no longer your style. You're not alone. Tens of thousands of students opt for an alternative Spring Break. Growing in popularity, alternative Spring Break trips are becoming quite the rage among college students.

What are they? Alternative Spring Breaks are something different from the customary "run to the beach and see how much I can drink before I throw up" trips. Alternative Spring Break vacations may be service-based or community-oriented. They may tackle social issues or offer leadership programs. You may be trading your bikini for a hammer and your flip-flops for work boots, but make no mistake, alternative Spring Break programs are an incredible opportunity to think less of yourself and more of your community and fellow man. They also look great on your resume. Check with your campus to see if they offer alternative Spring Break programs. Consider getting a group of friends together with whom to volunteer your time. Here are a few websites to get you started:

✓ www.alternativebreaks.org
✓ www.crossculturalsolutions.org
✓ www.springbreakalternative.org

6

Greek Life and Hazing

"But you can't hold a whole fraternity responsible for the behavior of a few, sick, twisted individuals. For if you do, then shouldn't we blame the whole fraternity system? And if the whole fraternity system is guilty, then isn't this an indictment of our educational institutions in general? I put it to you, Greg, isn't this an indictment of our entire American society? Well, you can do whatever you want to us, but we're not going to sit here and listen to you badmouth the United States of America. Gentlemen!"

The above proclamation was said by Tim Matheson, a.k.a. Otter, from a scene in the 1978 classic movie *Animal House*. In that scene, the Delta House fraternity was being reviewed at a conduct hearing to determine if the fraternity should have its charter revoked. Good or bad, the reputation of fraternities and sororities is the party life. Many people still conjure up images of the movie *Animal House* when they think of fraternities.

In recent years, fraternities have come under criticism for the practice of "hazing." However, hazing is not just limited to fraternities. Hazing incidents occur in the military and have been reported on high school and collegiate sports teams, cheerleading squads, and marching bands, although the practice is primarily associated with fraternities and sororities.

This is not to say that the Greek system is something that should be avoided. It's an individual preference whether or not to belong. Some find

Greek membership to be an enriching experience. Many fraternity brothers and sorority sisters develop a bond that can last a lifetime. Fraternities and sororities have also sponsored philanthropic events in their respective cities. In many towns, you can see Greeks on street corners collecting donations for various charities, such as the fight against cancer.

Fraternities are steeped in tradition. Phi Beta Kappa was the very first fraternity in the United States. It was founded in 1776 at the College of William and Mary in Williamsburg, Virginia. It was not long ago when fraternities were considered elitist organizations. Their reputation notwithstanding, presidents, Supreme Court Justices, inventors, Nobel Prize recipients, actors, world-class athletes, astronauts, CEOs, and a host of other leaders in their fields have all been members of fraternities and sororities.

Fraternities and sororities are an area of college life where not all students are members. On smaller campuses, the Greek system is minimized or even nonexistent. On midsize and large campuses, fraternities and sororities can play a central role in campus activities and university functions. Most students come in contact with these organizations at some point in their college life, and each year thousands of students across the country are recruited for membership. So, would a fraternity want you? Do you want them? If you do, you may have to prove yourself worthy.

So, What's the Rush?

Historically, rush week is when students would hurry to join a particular fraternity or sorority. Many times this was done in order to find housing. In the past, fraternity members actually rushed out to entice incoming freshmen before another fraternity on campus attracted them to join their organization. Typically, rush is a time of year fraternities and sororities set aside to recruit new members. Most recruitment drives today will last a few weeks instead of just one week. Members of fraternities and sororities will sponsor events such as barbecues, bowling outings, movie nights, and service-orientated projects to draw new members.

Members of the fraternities and sororities invite fellow students to attend these events as a way to meet members and learn more about their particular chapter. Once rush week is over, students will then *pledge* to a fraternity or sorority with whom they are comfortable. Many times, there is a pledging ceremony where students will express their interest in joining. Depending on the chapter, the pledge process normally lasts four to eight weeks. During that time, pledges may be required to pay dues and attend meetings. These meetings, usually secretive in nature, are the very foundation of the pledge process.

During the pledge process, the new members or pledges attend meetings to learn about the history of the fraternity. In the course of declaring a commitment, brothers may try to break a pledge, both physically and mentally. With such an overwhelming desire to belong, many pledges can be subjected to unimaginable treatment. Unfortunately, somewhere along the fraternity evolution, pledging one's commitment to the chapter became a test of wills to endure punishment all in the name of fraternal allegiance. Hazing is the cancer of fraternities and other groups that employ abuse to determine a candidate's dedication.

"Thank you sir, may I have another?" was the famous line Kevin Bacon said in the movie *Animal House* as he was being smacked unmercifully with a wooden paddle. Although Bacon, a pledge for Omega House, was in excruciating pain, he continued to ask for additional spankings as a way to show his dedication and loyalty to the brotherhood of the fraternity.

Hazing

Serious safety issues occur annually within the Greek community in regards to hazing and recruiting initiation practices. As a result, many people have dedicated their lives and careers to the prevention of hazing. From lobbying state lawmakers, developing websites, and speaking publicly on the subject, there is a concerted effort on many fronts to eliminate this practice.

One such organization is StopHazing.org, which was established in 1998 by two former students of the University of New Hampshire. Their website, www.StopHazing.org, provides up-to-date, accurate information for students, parents, and educators. The organization defines hazing as follows:

"Hazing refers to any activity expected of someone joining a group (or to maintain full status in a group) that humiliates, degrades or risks emotional and/or physical harm, regardless of the person's willingness to participate. Hazing activities are generally considered to be: physically abusive, hazardous, and/or sexually violating. The specific behaviors or activities within these categories vary widely among participants, groups and settings. While alcohol use is common in many types of hazing, other examples of typical hazing practices include: personal hygiene, yelling, swearing and insulting new members/rookies, being forced to wear embarrassing or humiliating attire in public, consumption of vile substances or smearing of such on one's skin, brandings, physical beatings, binge drinking and drinking games, sexual simulation and sexual assault."

Many other people and organizations are trying to curtail, if not eliminate, the hazing ritual altogether. Numerous books have also been written on the topic. Hank Newer, journalism professor at Indiana University, noted author, and leading expert on hazing said, "The prevalence of hazing is still very heavy, especially in terms of alcohol related incidents at fraternities. Hazing will not end in my lifetime. The momentum is there. It is such a problem in high schools and not being addressed, that it is carrying over into college. Until they stop it at the high school level, we're going to continue to see it being problematic."

Throughout this book, I have shared stories and suggested precautions as a way to minimize the risk of being injured while attending college. Because of the uniqueness of hazing, and the profound impact it has on the victim's family and the collegiate community, I thought there is no better way to demonstrate the harm hazing can do than to hear from the mother of a hazing victim.

For me to attempt to articulate the immense, life-altering pain a mother feels when she has lost her child would be inappropriate. To spend a minute talking with Debbie Smith is to realize what a remarkable person she is. Debbie is a person of strength, conviction, purpose, and forgiveness. I was privileged to spend time interviewing Debbie over the phone. I listened as she talked about her son, Matthew. I am truly honored that she agreed to share her story. I present an e-mail that Debbie Smith sent to me on, August 16, 2007.

It is so important that our young people and parents alike have a better understanding of what can happen when they go away to college. I only wish we had known what kinds of things go on so we could have taught Matt. I want to bring awareness of the hidden dangers out there masked behind brotherly and sisterly love and the desire to be accepted. It is so important to me that others learn by what happed to Matt, so that they, and their families do not have to suffer the way Matt suffered and the way we continue to suffer.

Matt would want others to be spared his fate because that is the person he was. As his mother, I have vowed to see what I know would be his wish, though in his memory. It helps me knowing that we may be able to save someone by telling Matt's story, and by doing this we are also keeping Matt's memory alive.

Out of respect for the Smith and Carrington families, I have chosen not to go into detail regarding the specific events that led up to the horrible day that took Matthew Carrington from his family and friends. Rather, I give to you a letter that Matt's mother read as an "impact statement" on the day Matt's fraternity brothers were sentenced to prison.

A HEARTBROKEN MOTHER

I was born to be a mother. I don't remember a time in my life growing up when I didn't want to have children. I tried for years before I found out that I would have to be artificially inseminated in order to have Matt. When preparing for my first insemination, I had been advised not to get too excited because it rarely took on the first try. But I was one of the lucky ones or so I thought. Less than three weeks after my first insemination I discovered I was pregnant. I was overjoyed, but it only lasted a short time and by the time I was eight weeks I had lost the baby.

After a miscarriage, bouts with depression and several more attempts, Matt was finally conceived. He was my little angel. He truly was my gift from God and that is where he got his name, Matthew, meaning a gift from God.

Matt was everything you could ever want in a son. He was sweet, loving, and thoughtful. He cared about everyone and their feelings. He always put everyone before himself. He was so selfless and giving he never wanted anyone to feel bad or left out. He was smart, so funny, and quick-witted. He was always up for anything no matter how lame or physically strenuous. He was an incredible athlete. There was nothing he couldn't do. I miss watching him play basketball and throw a Frisbee and a football. I miss he and his brother, Travis, playing catch with the baseball or playing basket-ball in the street while I am finishing up dinner and going out and telling them it's ready.

I miss coming around the corner and seeing his car in the front of the house and my heart skipping a beat because Matt is home and him calling out, "Hi Mom" and coming to the car to give me a big hug and kiss. I miss sitting on the couch with him and watching TV those nights until I couldn't stay awake any longer; only to get up a couple hours later to see that he is still flipping through the channels because he doesn't have cable in Chico and wants to get his fill in before finally falling asleep.

I miss talking to him on the phone for 45 minutes to an hour while he is running around in his car, going to the post office, the bank, walking around campus, or sitting in the drive thru. I miss having him surprise me at work and take me to lunch. I miss having him sit across the table at dinner and knowing that I will never make another meal for him. I miss hearing him say, "I love you, Mom." I miss his smiling face and loving heart.

I miss all the trips we will never take together again as a family. Matt loved spending time with the family. He would always rearrange his busy schedule to make sure he could make every trip, every Christmas, Thanksgiving, Easter, Mother's Day, Father's Day, every birthday, or just come home to spend the day or night. I miss his gifts. He was the greatest and most thoughtful gift giver. He always knew just what to get you, and you always looked forward to his presents. I miss that I will not get to throw him his college graduation party. I started planning in August 2004, a week after we moved him to Chico. We were all so proud of him; we knew how successful he was going to be.

What we have lost in Matt can never be replaced. As one of my nephews said, "He was the shining star of the cousins." Matt was the shining star of all of our lives. He was the one that we all aspired to be like. Everyone loved Matt, you couldn't help yourself. There was nothing not to love. Over 600 people came to his service to pay their respects and as his friend Andrew put it, those were only the ones that could make it. Imagine how many people would have been there if everyone that wanted to be there could have been.

Our lives have been shattered and will never be the same. I will never dance with him at his wedding. We will never see Matt become a father; he would have been an incredible father. Travis' children will never know their Uncle Matt. Their children will never grow up together hearing their parents kid each other about how they grew up and talking about things they did together. I will never get to hold Matt's children, my grandchildren, and see Matt in their precious faces. I'll never be able to say he looks just like you, or you used to do that when you were little.

So much has been taken from us not just in our everyday life, but also our future. Matt was meant for greatness and his potential in life was unlimited. He had the world at his feet and was so focused on his future. He was full of life and joy, the possibilities for Matt were endless, but that was taken from him and us.

The morning of Wednesday, February 2, 2005, will forever be imbedded in my memory as the most devastating day of my life. I will never forget getting the call from Greg, at 6:15 a.m. telling me that something had happened to Matt, that he was in a hospital in Chico, and we had to find him. My heart sank. I knew it was bad, I felt it. I knew that something very bad had happened to my baby as I cried out, "No, not Matt!" I quickly called 411 and asked for numbers of all the hospitals in Chico and got only one.

I called the number and explained that my son, Matt Carrington, was in a hospital in Chico but I wasn't sure which one, as this was the only number given to me. The person on the other end said that they were the only hospital in Chico and would see if he was there. Another person got on the phone and asked if I was alone and I began to cry more. I told her my other son is here, Matt's younger brother, he's 14. She said that I would need to speak to the doctor. At this point I screamed to Travis who was on the phone with Greg to tell Dad to come home, now.

When the doctor got on the line he said that Matt had been found in the basement of a frat house. He wasn't breathing when the paramedics got there and when he was brought to the hospital, he was in full arrest. He said he was in critical condition and to get to the hospital as soon as we could, but not to drive myself. I told him that my husband was on his way home from the city and should be here in about 20 or 30 minutes. I asked the doctor who was at the hospital with Matt and he said no one, that Matt was alone. I asked him to please do whatever he could to save Matt. My mind went crazy, "Alone!" why is he alone? Why isn't someone with him? What did they do to him? What could have possibly happened to my baby? What were they doing up at this time in the morning on a school night? What happened to Matt? I began to call numbers but couldn't reach anyone. Phones weren't being answered and when they were, they were going straight to voice mail. I called my friend Bobbie, and her husband, Bill. I had called Greg to tell him about Matt, but he had gotten a call from their daughter, Kristi in Merced who got a call from Mike Quintana. But Bobbie didn't know anything. I couldn't reach Kristi, but that didn't matter because she didn't know anything, either. Nobody knew anything, and all I knew is that my son was 3 hours away from home, alone in a hospital, possibly dying and I needed to get to him. He needed his mother.

Stephanie, a social worker, began calling me to make sure that I was okay. This set off alarms in my head. "Why is a social worker calling me?" I kept thinking. But nothing at this point mattered. All I knew was that I had to get to my baby, I had to be there with him, I had to hold him. He needed me, and I needed to be with him. I called my sister, Frankie, and told her that Matt was in the hospital in Chico in critical condition and we were leaving as soon as Greg got here. I told her it didn't sound good. She said I am leaving work and will meet you up there. Every minute seemed like 20, as Travis and I waited anxiously for

Greg to get home. My mind was going a million miles a minute, my despair was overwhelming. I tried to remember things I thought we might need because I didn't know how long we would be there. I told Travis to call his baseball coach because he would not be at practice. I told him to try to eat something because I didn't know when he would have that opportunity again, and it was a long drive. Get something warm, it will probably be cold there. We need water for the ride up. Get my phone charger from my car because the hospital has my number and I will need to stay in communication with them. Where is Greg? Why is he taking so long? Matt, Matt, what did they do to you? I need to be with Matt, he needs me. Where is Greg? Why isn't he here yet? We have to get to Matt. What happened? Why is he alone? He shouldn't be alone. Why isn't someone with him? I need to be with him, he needs me. Where's Greg? Travis call dad and see how much longer. Matt, Matt, I love you honey. Hang on, we're coming.

Stephanie continued to call me to see where we were and how we were doing. I told her that Greg was still on his way, but we should be on the road shortly. Finally, Greg pulled up. I called to Travis, "Dad is here. Let's go sweetie, we've got to get to Matt." We jumped in the truck and were on our way. We all wondered out loud what could have possibly happened. What were they doing down there? I thought the pledging was over? Why were they up at that time on a school night? Why wasn't someone with Matt? How could they leave him alone? Our sweet Matt, what did they do to you? We knew that it couldn't have been drugs or alcohol because Matt was too smart for that. We taught him at a young age the dangers of drugs and excess alcohol. What could it have been?

An hour and a half into the drive, with an hour and a half to go, Stephanie called again. I couldn't take it anymore. I told her I need to know what is going on with my son. I know it's bad. I need to know are we going to make it in time. I begged her to tell me the truth about my baby. She finally said, "We don't like to give this news over the phone." I began to cry and she said, "I'm sorry Debbie, Matt didn't make it." This scream came out of me from deep within my being, then, "No, not Matt!"

I don't know what happened with the phone at that point. Travis was crying behind me, and Greg was crying next to me and began to drive erratically. I couldn't reach Travis. I said, "Greg, pull off the freeway. We need to be together as a family." He pulled off and into a gas station parking lot where we all got out of the car and hugged each other in our traditional family hug, but this time without Matt. Our family hugs would never be the same. Oh God, not Matt. Not our sweet Matt. How could this happen? What could they have possible done to him?

When we arrived at the hospital and were finally taken to Matt, we were told before we could see him that we would not be able to touch him. I cried in pain, "What?" I need to hold my baby. Stephanie said that the coroner had to do an autopsy first so his body could not be disturbed. I turned and saw a covered body at the end of the room and said, "Is that Matt?" Stephanie said yes. My knees began to buckle. As we approached him I was hoping against hope that there had been a mistake, but something inside of me felt that my sweet baby boy was really gone. As we got closer, I saw his right arm, which was not covered and I began to shake. Oh God, Matt's arm. As Stephanie slowly pulled the sheet from his head, I saw his perfect hair and began to weep. Matt! I need to touch him, I have to hold him, he's my baby. He had tubes coming out of him and blood and something else all over. He was a mess and they wouldn't let me hold him. He had to lay there all alone. He had been alone way too long. I didn't want to leave him like that. I wanted to take care of him but they wouldn't let me. There was nothing that I could do. Then I remembered that Travis had gone back to the grieving room because he didn't want to see Matt like that and I needed to get to him. He needed me, too.

After speaking with the police, we went back to Matt's house where I crawled into his unmade bed, covered myself with his blankets and the clothes he had changed out of before he left. I breathed in Matt. My baby is gone, what will we do without him? How will our perfect family go on? Will we ever be the perfect family again? Will we ever be the same? What do we do next?

I cry uncontrollably everyday for my precious son. Some days are so bad it will just go on for hours. I hate that the last three days of Matt's life were so torturous. I hate that I was not there to protect him as I had his whole life. My pain is so great that at times I don't know how I am going to make it. I just want Matt back so badly; I want my family back the way it was, perfect, but I know that is something that will never happen. My life will never be the same, our life will never be the same. Life, as we knew it, is gone forever.

I know that Matt's death was never intended, and I believe or hope that those involved are very sorry for what they did. But because of their actions and selfishness, a sweet and selfless boy is gone forever. And for their actions, they must be punished. This is how we teach our children right from wrong. I hope that whatever their punishment is, they learn from it and their actions the morning of February 2, and become better people for it. I hope that they will want to teach others from their mistakes by telling their story about how they took the life of such a wonderful person they called 'brother' and letting them know how wrong they were so that other lives can be saved. Through this, maybe we can someday put a stop to hazing altogether.

*　　*　　*

Matt Carrington was a pledge for the Chi Tau Fraternity. As was custom, the hazing took place in the cold, wet, sewer-infested basement of the frat house. His mother Debbie said, "He was terribly degraded and mistreated for the last three days of his life, all for the purpose of gaining admission into the fraternity, demonstrating his worthiness, and satisfying the brotherly love that the fraternity members promoted."

Without question, the majority of deaths from fraternity hazing incidents involve alcohol. Matthew Carrington did not die of alcohol poisoning. As a matter of fact, the autopsy revealed that Matt had no alcohol or drugs in his body. Matt Carrington died of water intoxication! As part of the hazing ritual and pledge process, Matt's fraternity brothers forced him to drink large quantities of water, while other despicable acts were thrust upon him.

Hazing has destroyed numerous lives and has shattered families. The notion of being degraded or injured in order to be accepted is ludicrous. Regrettably, by the time most students realize what is happening, they have already been sucked in by the fraternal vortex, and it's too late. Take a minute, and visit the website created to honor Matthew Carrington. You will be glad you did: www.wemissyoumatt.com.

I CAN HAVE TOO MUCH WATER?

Yes, you can! Although nothing is better to hydrate our bodies than water, too much water, in a short amount of time cannot only hurt you, but can kill you. Water intoxication, or hyponatremia, is caused by drinking large quantities of water in a short amount of time, thereby diluting the amount of sodium or salt in your blood, causing an electrolyte imbalance that can result in death.

It is not uncommon for water intoxication conditions to be present in infants. The condition is also found in athletes who run marathons or any athlete who sweats heavily. If the electrolytes are not replenished, and water is still being consumed, water intoxication can occur. Signs of water intoxication can include the following:

✓ Light-headedness
✓ Nausea
✓ Vomiting
✓ Confusion
✓ Headache
✓ Fatigue
✓ Cramping
✓ Seizures

Never allow anyone to force large quantities of water on you. Most people are not aware that a person can die from water intoxication. Matthew Carrington should have never died that February morning. Joining a fraternity or sorority is an individual decision. Whether you decide to pledge or not, there may be an occasion when you attend a fraternity party or Greek-sponsored event. Here are some suggestions to keep you as safe as possible.

✓ Know your drinking limitations. Because it's much less expensive to attend a fraternity party than an off-campus nightclub, you may be tempted to drink more than you had intended.

✓ Don't participate in binge drinking activities such as beer-bongs or drinking a predetermined number of shots of liquor in a specified time.

✓ Always maintain your moral standards when you are pledging.

✓ Don't partake in any activity that could risk injury. Hazing can be deadly.

✓ Try to find out the reasons why other people backed out or were not accepted at a particular house.

✓ Ask yourself before you do anything, "Could this harm me in any-way?" Chances are if you even have to ask yourself that question, you probably should not be doing the activity.

✓ Never set your drink down and walk away.

✓ Do not accept a drink from anyone you don't know.

✓ If you are partying in a house, don't go to a member's room alone.

✓ If you feel you are being degraded by doing an activity, even for a little while, you are being hazed.

StopHazing.org lists the following advice about the myths and facts regarding hazing.

Myth: Hazing is primarily a problem for fraternities and sororities.

Fact: Hazing is a societal problem. Hazing incidents have been frequently documented in a variety of clubs and organizations, including the military, athletic teams, marching bands, religious cults, and professional schools. Reports of hazing activities in high schools are on the rise.

Myth: Hazing is no more than foolish pranks that sometimes go awry.

Fact: Hazing is an act of power and control over others—it is victimization. Hazing is pre-meditated and *not* accidental.

Hazing is abusive, degrading, and often life threatening.

Myth: As long as there's no malicious intent, a little hazing should be okay.

Fact: Even if there's no malicious intent, safety may still be a factor in traditional hazing activities that are considered to be all in good fun. For example, serious accidents have occurred during scavenger hunts and kidnapping trips. Besides, what purpose do such activities serve in promoting the growth and development of group team members?

Myth: Hazing is an effective way to teach respect and develop discipline.

Fact: First of all, respect must be earned—not taught. Victims of hazing rarely report having respect for those who have hazed them. Just like other forms of victimization, hazing breeds mistrust, apathy, and alienation.

Myth: If someone agrees to participate in an activity, it can't be considered hazing.

Fact: In states that have laws against hazing, consent of the victim can't be used as a defense in a civil suit. This is because even if someone agrees to participate in a potentially hazardous action, it may not be true consent when considering peer pressure and desire to belong to the group.

Myth : It's difficult to determine whether or not a certain activity is hazing—it's such a grey area sometimes.

Fact: It's not difficult to decide if an activity is hazing if you use common sense and ask yourself the following questions:

Make the following inquiries of each activity to determine whether or not it is hazing.
1. Is alcohol involved?
2. Will active/current members of the group refuse to

participate [in the activity that the pledges] are being asked to do?

3. Does the activity risk emotional or physical damage?

4. Is there risk of injury or a question of safety?

5. Do you have any reservation describing the activity to your parents, a professor, or a university official?

6. Would you object to the activity being photographed for the school newspaper or filmed by the local TV news crew?

If the answer to any of these questions is yes, the activity is probably hazing.

Fraternity Fires

Every year fires strike off-campus student residences. According to the Center for Campus Fire Safety, 11 percent of all fatal fires were in fraternities and sororities. Many Greek residences are older structures that lack automatic sprinkler systems. Alcohol consumption also played a major role in the off-campus fatalities.

If you're considering moving into Greek housing, it's important to keep fire safety as a top priority. Recognize that the wiring could be outdated and not meet current building codes. Be certain to check smoke alarms and know all escape routes. If possible, request to have a room with a window. Even if it's on the upper floors, having a room with a window is better than a room with no window. Stay alert on party nights. With possibly hundreds of students drinking alcohol at a fraternity party, it can create a dangerous situation. Arson is still the number one cause of all fires, both on and off campus. Think about these fire safety precautions if you move into Greek housing.

✓ Exit the building immediately should you hear any fire alarm.

✓ You need to have at least two escape routes when exiting your room in the fraternity house.

✓ Check the fire extinguishers and make sure they are in proper working order.

✓ Double-check all smoke alarms. Ask if they are hard-wired and tied together.

✓ Purchase a UL-listed smoke alarm and CO2 detector for your individual room; products are available online or at any home improvement store.

I Owe More Than
My School Loans

I'll Just Put It on My Card

No, no, no. Let someone else put the bill on *their* card. Nellie Mae, the largest provider of student loans, published a report in May 2005. The report stated, "76 percent of undergraduates in 2004 began the school year with credit cards. And the average outstanding balance on undergraduate credit cards was $2,169." That's not a good thing!

Without question, when credit cards are used responsibly, they are a wonderful tool and can be very helpful. Credit cards are an ideal way to establish good credit with credit bureau agencies, and they're great for emergencies. This could include a medical emergency or flying home at the last minute due to an urgent situation. Having a car repaired is yet another unforeseen expense. However, buying a new outfit does *not* constitute an emergency. I know what you're thinking, but it really doesn't.

Credit cards are a double-edged sword. Like most good things, there's a downside. Unfortunately, the downside to credit card debt can literally last a lifetime. You can drown in a sea of debt. It's smothering! If you use credit cards irresponsibly, it can do a great deal of harm even years after you graduate. Getting sucked into the credit card vortex is easily done, but it can be extremely difficult to get out. It can also hurt you while you're in school. The pressure to pay off high credit card balances while attending college can be overwhelming to the point where you focus on getting jobs to pay off the balance rather than focusing on your studies.

Don't feel bad. Many families today are struggling with their own finances. Families with salaries, mortgages, and children have difficulty managing credit cards.

So how can you overcome the credit card trap? It's important to recognize how this happens in the first place. You will be inundated by credit card companies as soon as you arrive on campus. Credit card offers will occur almost daily, not only in person, but by mail. The U.S. Department of Education reported that almost half of all college students receive credit card applications on a daily or weekly basis.

As you are walking around campus, you'll notice people sitting behind a table asking you to fill out an application for a credit card. They're everywhere! You don't have to do anything else. It all starts off innocently enough. You're full of good intentions and rationalize that you will be very responsible, so you begin filling out the application.

A few weeks pass until your card arrives in the mail. You're proud of your card as you have matured into the world of financial plastic. You tuck it away for now and don't give it too much thought. Similar to other college students, you're tight on cash. Your parents helped you layout a budget prior to getting on campus, but you always seem to come up short at the end of the month. Don't worry, I'm not faulting you for buying that sweatshirt last week. You need to show your support for the football team. And how could you have possibly missed the victory celebration after the game?

As the end of the week nears, you realize it's been a killer semester. You have just finished two of the most difficult tests you've ever taken, and it's time to celebrate. Since you're tired of the cafeteria food, this is a perfect time to break in the new credit card and treat yourself to a decent dinner. Being fiscally responsible, you don't want to spend a lot, so you decide you will head off campus to a casual pub known for its great dinner specials and wonderful salads.

As you and your roommate begin to unwind, two people from your dorm happen to show up at the restaurant. They, too, had the same tough tests as you, and everyone begins to analyze the crazy questions. They each order a drink, and the waitress asks, "Shall I start a tab?" "Sure, that sounds great," you say.

This restaurant may be known for its dinner specials and salads, but it's also a place other students like to visit. Within the next hour, eight more students you know are hanging out just having a few drinks. Everyone takes their turn buying rounds, but since your credit card was the first tab started, it's the largest bill at the end of the night. What you thought was going to be a bill for $38.50 is now $198.

Since you've been a little cash strapped lately, and it's running late, you suggest to everyone, "Just pay me, and I'll keep it on my card." Your friends begin to fork over their portion of the bill. With a belly full of food, a complicated exam behind you, and $160 cash in your pocket, you're quite satisfied when you leave the restaurant.

Typically, credit card spending in college is not tied to educational purposes. Most credit card debt is a lifestyle issue. If you have a credit card or are planning on getting one, determine what it's going to be used for. Ask yourself, "Why do I need this? What will I purchase?" Credit cards are astonishingly easy to obtain, but very difficult to manage. There's no question they're tempting. For some students, applying for a credit card may prove too much of a temptation to resist.

Budgeting money while you're in school and trying to save a few dollars can become quite a challenge for even disciplined students. One of the biggest financial challenges you'll face in college, other than your student loan, is credit card debt. If not managed properly, credit card debt can make you a slave to minimum payments and incessant late fees. The consequences of credit card debt can be life altering. Don't get sucked into the thought process of, "If my interest rate was lower, I could handle the payment."

It's not uncommon for students who are behind on one card to open another and transfer the first balance to the new card because the interest rate is lower. They get behind on the second one and open a third. If this happens, stop! Don't open any more cards. As a matter of fact, get a pair of scissors and cut up the ones you already have. The notion of having multiple cards is a farce. No one has ever explained to me why anyone *needs* multiple credit cards. In case you're wondering, yep, just one. It works everywhere, every time I need it.

You will also begin to notice something. Your mailbox will be full of new credit card offers with amazing low rates. Teaser rates they're called. More times than not, these low rates are limited to a short amount of time and then the rates will skyrocket. Credit card interest can crush you. I like to call it legal loan sharking. With most rates in the 18 to 22 percent range, and some at 24 percent, it can literally take a lifetime to pay off your debt. The credit card companies are banking (pun intended) that you will just pay the minimum balance. Why do you think they are soliciting you in the first place? If every person who held a credit card paid it in full, the card companies would not make any money. That's why they love college students. Isn't it great to be loved for something?

✎ Hot Tip:
If you cannot pay your credit card off in full, each and every month, you can't afford the purchase.

It's easy for me to say, I guess because I'm writing the book, but you *must* live within your means. I know that sounds harsh, but did you ever wonder why college students live on macaroni and cheese? Here's another classic but flawed thought process that many students live by: "I realize I owe thousands of dollars on my credit card, but I'll just pay it off when I get my first job. After all, the starting salary in my field is over thirty thousand." Oh, to be young again. Listen, we'll talk about budgeting in a few minutes.

The financial burden of credit card debt is just the beginning of a vicious cycle. Please, if you get in over your head, let your parents know. Yes, they may not be happy. But your parents may be able to increase your payments, or pay off your balance all together. Perhaps you can wash their car for the next ten years if you promise never to buy another thing. If for some reason, you're uncomfortable telling your parents, you should consider seeking advice from a professional debt counselor.

Okay, let's say you miss a couple of payments, just by accident. Yes, the collection calls will begin. Now you start screening your phone calls. You live by caller ID to screen the collector's calls. Pretty soon, you don't enjoy receiving your mail because it's full of past-due collection notices. Your financial affairs begin to spiral out of control. It doesn't sound pleasant does it? If you begin to fall behind and neglect a few payments on your credit card, some of the following will happen. It's simply not worth the damage it causes.

✓ Depending on the credit limit you have and how much you owe, credit card debt can negatively affect your credit report and credit score.

✓ If you apply for a car loan or restructure a student loan, your interest rates will be higher and in some cases you may not qualify at all.

✓ If your credit score is damaged due to credit card debt, employers may pass on hiring you over someone who has demonstrated better money-management skills.

✓ Applications for apartments may be rejected or require substantial security deposits due to credit card debt.

✓ Insurance rates may increase due to credit card debt.

✓ Opening multiple card accounts will lower your credit score.

✓ Constantly switching your cards to receive lower interest rates will lower your score.

If you ever find yourself in a situation similar to the student who put the entire dinner bill on his credit card consider doing this: tell the server you just want *your portion* on the card. The server will happily accommodate your request. Everybody pays their fair share in cash, and you are only putting the thirty bucks you owe on the card.

Many young folks with credit cards are also under the impression that when someone requests to "validate your card," that the purchase must remain on the card. It's simply not so. Let's say you check into a hotel. The front desk clerk will invariably ask you, "Sir, I'll need to validate your credit card." Without thinking, you pull out your card, and the clerk runs it through the computer. You can inform the clerk at that point that you'd prefer to pay cash. The clerk will tell you that it's not a problem and simply inform the person behind the desk when you check out.

If your credit card is ever lost or stolen, do not panic. As long as you notified the card company, you will not be liable for unauthorized charges. Under the Federal Trade Commission's Fair Credit Billing Act, federal law limits your responsibility to fifty dollars for any unauthorized charges. Follow these guidelines to ensure that your credit card remains safe:

- ✔ If you lose your credit card or think it was stolen, notify your credit card company immediately. The customer service phone number can be found on your last statement.
- ✔ There have been reports of thieves calling the victim to say they found your purse or wallet, and they'll return everything to you. This strategy, although not often used, can give the criminal a day or two to charge many purchases on the card before you actually cancel it.
- ✔ Never give your credit card number over the phone unless it is a very reputable company with a long track record.
- ✔ Use caution when purchasing anything online. No one should ever ask for your Social Security number when using a credit card. If they do, report them immediately.
- ✔ Keep your credit card in a very secure place. Treat it like cash.
- ✔ If the store or restaurant you're visiting still uses carbon paper copies, make sure you take the carbon and tear them up.
- ✔ If you receive any e-mail notification asking you to "verify" account numbers or PIN numbers, do not respond back. Call your bank or credit card company and ask if they e-mailed anything to you.
- ✔ When you receive credit card offers in the mail, and you will, shred or destroy the application. Do not just toss it in the trash can.

There Must Be Another Way

There is, lucky you. Using a debit card can be a great alternative to credit cards. Debit cards limit you to the amount of money that's in your bank or credit union account. You simply deposit the money you have available with your bank. Whenever you make a purchase, the funds are automatically withdrawn from your account. If the green stuff isn't in your bank account, sorry, no sweatshirt for you.

Another beautiful thing about debit cards is you will never have interest charges or late fees. Some banks may charge a small service fee, but it's nothing like late payments. Visa and MasterCard also offer prepaid cards. They are accepted anywhere and are similar in function to a bank debit card. When you're running low on your card, just reload them and you're good to go. If there's a negative to debit cards, it's that they don't build any credit history with the credit bureaus. But don't worry about it—you have a long life ahead of you with ample time to build as much credit as you need.

Clearly, it's a personal choice whether or not you choose to have a credit card, debit card, or opt to pay cash. Anytime you're dealing with financial issues, no matter how big or small, precautions must be considered.

Many of the topics in this book discuss how you can become the victim of a crime or an accident through no fault of your own. Someone could steal your laptop or your bike. You could be caught in a fire in a dorm or end up being assaulted during Spring Break. You didn't ask for any of those things to happen. Often, these events are completely out of your control.

Credit card debt is different. It's not random. It's not forced. It's one of the only safety issues I discuss in this book in which you have complete control. Debt is brought on by you. Only you can control credit cards, don't let them control you!

Picture Yourself on a Budget

No matter how old you are or what phase of life you're in, you need to have a budget, even if your parents are subsidizing you. Now, at the risk of having you roll your eyes at me, let's first talk about what a budget is. A budget is an itemized summary of what you *need* to live on versus what you *want* to live on and the amount of money coming in to support those needs and wants. Complicated stuff to be sure. In other words, don't spend more than you have.

I know what you're thinking, "So how do I know the amount of money I'll need?" How the heck do I know! Great answer huh? The answer is related in large part to the phase of life you're in at the present time. If you're living in the dorms, your budget will be different from someone who is living in an apartment. Once you leave school and you're on your own, your budget will be different from someone who is married with two children and a mortgage. Hopefully, with each one of those pivotal changes in your life, your income will match accordingly.

A budget is your financial plan in motion. Life changes and unforeseen things will happen, both good and bad. You need to remain flexible and adjust your budget to the *needs* (fixed costs) in your life, first, and the *wants* (variable costs) in your life, second. Determining those needs is just a function of sitting down and thinking about it. Everybody is different, but you can use this as a guide. Fill in the blanks with the best figures or estimates you have for each category.

Dorm Fixed Costs:

CATEGORY	COSTS
Tuition	$_____
Room and Board	$_____
Vehicle Payment	$_____
Insurance	$_____
Parking	$_____

Dorm Variable Costs:

Books	$_____
Cell phone	$_____
Clothes	$_____
Toiletries	$_____
Gasoline	$_____
Entertainment	$_____
Miscellaneous	$_____

If you're living in an apartment, most of the items above are still present, while others change. Apartment roommates can cause budgeting difficulties if someone moves out unexpectedly. You're now responsible for their share of the rent, in addition to any unpaid utilities. If that happens, your budget must change accordingly.

<u>CATEGORY</u>	<u>COSTS</u>
Rent	$_____
Utilities	$_____
Groceries	$_____
Transportation	$_____
Maintenance	$_____
Security deposits	$_____

Disciplining yourself to become a frugal shopper doesn't mean you're cheap. Shop within your budget. If you must have something, wait until it goes on sale. If you're considering a new cell phone, wait until your plan expires and then shop for the best package. Many times you can get a free phone by doing so.

✓ Open up a checking and savings account. Balance your accounts as soon as you receive the statements.

✓ Going out to eat on a regular basis can become quite expensive. Can you imagine paying for your two slices of pizza and soda for years to come if you put in on your credit card?

✓ Split a load of laundry with your roommate.

✓ If you do secure a part-time job, exercise restraint if you work at a clothing store. Many students will spend their entire paycheck on clothes without considering their other needs. Before you consider a job, make certain that your class and study schedule can handle it.

✓ Get in the habit of paying for everything with cash.

Your financial maturity is primarily based on how well you're able to budget and manage your finances. It takes time and effort. You will make mistakes. Nevertheless, by giving your finances the attention they deserve, you will put yourself on the path to financial freedom.

My Identity Can Be Stolen?

Each year, more than nine million Americans will have their identity stolen, according to the Federal Trade Commission. The U.S. Department of Education calls identity theft "one of the fastest growing consumer crimes in the nation." As a college student, you must handle your personal information with great care.

WHAT IS IDENTITY THEFT?

I know what you're thinking. "I don't have a lot of money, so why would they want me?" An identity thief does not want your money, he wants your name and reputation so he can *assume* your identity. Once the thief has your name, address, and Social Security number, he'll apply for a few address changes and, "Voila!" he has your identity. This can happen very fast. Identity thieves will apply for credit cards and possibly loans in your name and then go have a blast, all at your expense.

Let's say a thief doesn't want the hassle of filling out forms and changing addresses. It's extra work, right? They don't like the additional work, or they would not be stealing in the first place. If they get your personal information, they can order things instantaneously! Even if the credit card company picks up some superfluous charges and contacts you, it's too late. Now, you will not be responsible for the charges, but, oh, what a time you are going to have to straighten everything out. In other words, the identity thief is using *you* to commit fraud.

HOW DOES IT HAPPEN?

Think about the past week or past month. Chances are you've been to the store a few times. Did you write a check? Did you use a credit card? Did you order anything online? Have you taken advantage of a low-interest credit card offer? Did you go to the grocery store? Did you purchase a new cell phone or buy birthday presents for a family member? Did you use an ATM? Have you received any mail lately?

Every transaction you make, you reveal or disclose small bits of personal information. Some transactions require more information than others. If an identity thief is lucky enough to get your name, address, and Social Security number, it's similar to hitting 777 on a slot machine in Vegas.

Think about this scenario. You're at a football game, and you notice a table with two people, a lot of clipboards, and a free T-shirt offer for just filling out the application. At some sporting events, there are multiple tables on different levels of the stadium. The atmosphere is festive, busy, and noisy. Many students are filling out applications as the two behind the table call to you like an auctioneer. "Fill out the application and get a free T-shirt!" As you step up, they hand you a clipboard and pen with the application already attached. They're very helpful, aren't they?

You don't have to be at a football game. The minute you step on campus you will be inundated with people trying to get you to fill out an application for their credit card. Do you know these people behind the table? Do you know how careful they are with the application you just filled out?

Even if a clipboard and application are facing the two employees behind the table, I'll bet you the price of this book that a thief could read your name and Social Security number upside down. I would also bet you that a skilled identity thief could memorize your information rather quickly. They only need to be correct one time to steal a great deal of money.

The tables on campus or at a game are just one way to obtain your information. Thieves also use a variety of other methods to steal your identity. It's important to note, identity thieves do not need all your information. Just pieces will do. A thief may have someone on the *inside* who will literally give them or sell them your information. They may also get back to basics and just steal it. Purses and wallets are stolen every day. Your mail or checks may be stolen, including bank statements. Good old-fashioned dumpster diving is still a time-honored tradition. Because college students receive so many credit card offers each week, it doesn't take long before a thief hits pay dirt by going through your garbage. Again, shred or rip in pieces any credit card offers you receive in the mail.

But wait, there's more! Every day is another opportunity for identity thieves to conjure up new schemes. Here are a few classics that are used regularly.

- ✓ **Skimming**. Be careful using an ATM with a small box on the outside and a note telling you to swipe your card to gain access. The box is a data-storage device and will capture your banking information. Skimming can also be done in stores. Your credit card could be easily swiped by a separate box and then re-swiped in the legitimate register. If you're not paying attention, your information is gone.
- ✓ Thieves may complete a change-of-address form to redirect your mail to a different location.
- ✓ **Phishing**. It's an e-mail scam. Someone will send you an e-mail falsely claiming to be a bank or another legitimate organization. Yes, it does look real. Have you ever received an e-mail or a pop-up from a "bank" or financial institution requesting personal information? Never give any personal information that is requested online. Even if you think it's legitimate, call the bank directly before giving it to them.
- ✓ You may get a phone call at home or on your cell phone. The person calling will have a wonderful script and tell you he's either from a research firm or has an offer for you. He is doing this to obtain personal information about you. Give him nothing! Ask for his phone number and tell him you'll call him back.
- ✓ How about this one—you're standing in line at a store checking out, the cashier is patiently waiting, and the person behind you is waiting as he's talking on his cell phone. Everything appears fine as you're writing the check and hand the cashier your driver's license. The cashier hands you the receipt, and you're on your way. The guy behind you just bought a pack of gum. Instead of talking on the phone, he was taking multiple pictures of your check and driver's license. He's got what he needs.

Think all this may sound farfetched? Think again. According to the U.S. Department of Education, identity theft costs victims over five billion dollars annually. Over 9.9 million consumers were victims of identity theft in 2003 alone. If someone steals your identity, you will have a mess on your hands unlike anything you ever imagined. Why? Because only *you* can restore your good name. You will be solely responsible for reestablishing your identity and credit. It will cost you both time and money to reestablish your name and good credit standing. The FTC estimates it could cost you a few hours of time or hundreds of hours of time. Additionally, their findings say it may cost you nothing or over $1,000 to rectify the problem.

Identity theft is a federal crime. Although everyone is susceptible, the age group who is most at risk is *you!* The federal government states that eighteen- to twenty-nine-year-olds had the highest identity theft complaints in 2005. While there are masses of people and companies trying to curb the fraud, it's increasingly difficult to catch the perpetrators due to the creativity of the thieves. It's vital that you take an active role in protecting your information. Here are suggestions to minimize your risk.

- ✓ Protect your Social Security number like a mother bear protects her cubs! Ask why they need it. Ask how they will use it. Ask how they will protect it. Ask if you can give them another piece of information. Ask what happens if you don't give it to them.
- ✓ Guard all of your personal information. Name, address, bank accounts, employer, and most importantly, your Social Security number.
- ✓ Protect your computer system. Never answer e-mails from anyone saying they are your bank or others requesting personal information.
- ✓ Use caution throwing out trash. Shred or rip up credit card offers, receipts, insurance information, physician information, and bank statements.
- ✓ Always review your bank statements and credit card statements as soon as they are received.
- ✓ Ask questions yourself. Get tough! Ask them why they need the information they are requesting. If you don't like the answer, speak to a supervisor, or do not do business with them.

✔ Use caution while shopping.

✔ Check your credit report at least once a year.

I Have a Credit Report?

Yes, you do. Whether you realize it or not, by the time you've arrived on campus to begin your freshman year, more than likely, you have established a preliminary credit record with the credit bureau agencies. Student loans, cell phone applications, credit card accounts, and utility payments are only part of the credit profile a credit-reporting agency could have on file. Even if everything is in your parent's name, you still have a credit report listing your name, address, Social Security number, and your last job.

As the old saying goes, "The best things in life are free." Once each year, you're entitled to a free credit report from each of the major credit reporting agencies. The free reports were initially phased in when the federal Fair Credit Reporting Act was enacted. As of September 1, 2005, every American is entitled to a free report once each year.

Most importantly, every student should pull a credit report on themselves. By reviewing your credit report, you're able to establish a *baseline* and correct any problems that may be listed on the report. When speaking of finances in any forum, your credit report and credit score are king. The definitive word when dealing with credit reports is *correct*. Is the information about you on the reports correct?

Credit bureau agencies have had a long history of reports being incorrect. It may not be entirely their fault though. The credit bureaus are the receiving house for the lenders who provide the information to them. But make no mistake, they can be wrong.

We talked earlier in this chapter about identity theft and that the number one age group most at risk to have their identities stolen is your group—between eighteen and twenty-nine years old. There are many reasons for this, but two motivating factors for the crooks are that they know you probably have a careless attitude towards your credit, and because you have limited or no credit to speak of. They know your report is relatively "clean." Combine a relaxed attitude with a clean report, and you're an identity thief's dream. Order your credit report to verify that no one has stolen your identity and that the information they have on file is correct.

✎ Hot Tip:
Order your credit reports each summer before the beginning of school.

The ideal time to pull your reports is the summer before you return to school. If there are discrepancies, this will allow you the time to notify the credit bureau agencies in private and to rectify the situation in private. The last thing you need is a dorm full of people or the guys in your apartment hovering over you as you are dealing with a personal financial matter. Another bonus about receiving your reports in the summer is that it enables you to leave the reports at home with your parents.

Maintaining good credit during your college years and later in life is paramount to a successful financial future. If negative information is on your report, and it's correct, it will remain on your report for seven years before it's deleted. If you file bankruptcy, your negative information will stick with you for ten years.

The information contained in your report will have a direct impact, good or bad, on various aspects of your life. Automobile loans, home loans, and career opportunities can all be affected by your credit standing. Not only will lenders evaluate different pieces of your report to determine your credit worthiness, prospective employers will, too. The rationale companies give for doing this varies. Some want to verify that the information you put down on your application is consistent with the credit report. Others claim it's part of their background investigation. Many organizations want to get a handle as to your financial maturity.

Whatever their motive, be assured that businesses will pull your credit report. The competition for corporate positions and other professions is tough enough. As a job applicant, don't wait for a prospective employer to pull your report first. Know what's in your report before you apply for a job. By following these brief guidelines, your credit report will maintain a high rating.

✔ Pay all your bills on time, including utility bills.

✔ If you think you're going to be late, call the creditors and advise them of your situation.

✔ Keep your creditors to a minimum. Don't open multiple accounts.

✔ Keep the outstanding debt you have to a minimum. Credit card balances should be no more than 20-25 percent of the high limit.

✔ Immediately correct any inaccuracies in your credit report.

There are a few ways to obtain your free credit reports. You can order the reports directly from the three biggest reporting agencies. Their phone numbers and websites are below. You can visit, www.annualcreditreport.com and order them through this site. Check your report thoroughly, including your name, address, Social Security number, previous address, places of employment, and of course, your creditors. Make sure the lender account numbers listed coincide with the numbers you have at home. If you find an error, you must dispute your claim directly with the reporting agency.

✔ Equifax, 1-800-685-1111, www.equifax.com

✔ Transunion, 1-877-322-8228, www.transunion.com

✔ Experian, 1-888-397-3742, www.experian.com

My Credit Gets Scored?

Indeed it does! I just hope it's higher than your latest chemistry score. Actually, the grade analogy is not that far from reality, so let's go with it. Depending on your professor, he or she may grade you on a variety of factors. For example class attendance, test scores, class participation, and homework are a few ways a professor may calculate your grade.

One professor may value those areas very highly and consider your final exam an equal portion of your final grade, while another professor may put little emphasis on those areas and may consider your final exam of greatest importance.

Your credit score is based solely on information contained in your credit report. No, there is no mystical credit professor you can speak with to plead your case. "Really Credit Professor, I know I've been three months behind on my credit card payments, but my car payments are finally caught up. I promise, I won't be late again!" That may work with your English Literature professor, but it's not going to work here.

Many factors are considered when calculating your score. Let's break it down while keeping in mind the comparison of the professor giving you your final grade at the end of the semester.

1. Have you paid your bills on time? If you have, you get an "A," if not, you get an "F." Tricky isn't it? Your past payment history is a large portion of that calculation given the fact that a lender wants to see if the odds are good that he will be repaid.

2. How much outstanding debt do you have? For example, if your credit card has a credit limit of $2,500 and you owe $2,400, you'll probably get an "F." However, if you only owe $275.00 on that credit card, you would receive an "A." It's similar with a house or car loan. Let's say your car is $15,000, but you put nothing down and you owe $14,150. You're kind of maxed out, aren't you?

3. How old are you? This one may be unfair, but essentially they value the length of time you've had credit given to you. Since you're in college, you haven't had credit too long. It's really not about your age. A better question is how long have you had established credit?

4. How many credit cards have you applied for? Your credit score factors in how many times companies have "pulled" your report, or made an inquiry. If you have applied for five credit cards in the past six months, an "F." If you've had the same card for three years and have not applied for anything else, an "A." By applying for a lot of credit cards or loans, it signals to the lender that you may be in a financial pickle.

5. What kind of credit do you have? Isn't it all the same? Well, yes . . . and no. Envision this, someone hands you a bunch of money, all

bills. You have a wad of one-dollar bills, a few twenty-dollar bills, and two fifty-dollar bills. Technically, it's all money, but the value on each is different. Let's say you have a number of consumer loans or credit cards. You also have your school loan. Since your job is going well, you want to buy a house or get a home loan. Just don't load yourself down with an abundance of one-dollar bills or consumer loans.

So back to your chemistry score. If the test is worth 100 points, and you received a 60, well, you know the answer. Credit scores range from 300 to 850. If we were to correlate the 60 you received on the chemistry test to a credit score, your credit score would be about a 475. It's not good. Ideally, you'd like your score to be over 700 at all times. That equates to a solid "B."

8

Wheels on Campus

In our society, cars, bicycles, buses, motorcycles, and good old foot power are the basic modes of transportation. On college campuses, it's no different. Although cars have become much more prevalent on college campuses than ten years ago, students lucky enough to have one are still in the minority.

Most colleges have very specific policies relating to vehicles on campus. Some will not issue permits to freshmen, while others are more liberal. Nevertheless, one thing is for sure, the student who has a car will be very popular.

An argument could also be made that having a car on campus could actually keep you safer. You know that you're a very responsible driver. Bumming rides from other students, who may not be as responsible, might pose an increased danger. You also know that you would never drive a car under the influence of alcohol. As a matter of fact, it may be a plus to be the one with the car because it enables you to truthfully tell your peers, "I'm the designated driver."

Other positions could be taken to justify your reason for having a car on campus. However, bringing a vehicle of any kind to college is an individual family decision. That decision is also predicated on the college's policies. Before you run to your parents and say, "Mom and Dad, the guy who wrote this book said I should have a car on campus," let's first look at how the majority of students will be getting around.

Good Old Foot Power

Have you heard the stories that some older folks tell about going to school? "We walked three miles to school each way in the snow—and it was uphill both ways!" And they were just talking about the third grade. Whether you have a car on campus or a bicycle, you will still spend the majority of your time walking. I mean *a lot* of walking.

There are certainly many benefits to walking. Most noticeable, it's free. There are no fuel costs, no parking costs, and no maintenance costs. Many college campuses can become very congested with normal everyday traffic. Between the college staff, neighboring employees, and local town folks, driving on campus can become a challenge, as well as a test of patience. As you will come to learn, it's not unusual for you to make it to your destination faster by foot than by car.

College life is a time for you to evolve. Unfortunately, with no parents around to oversee your eating habits, your waistline may also begin to change. The dreaded *freshman 15* is a term given to many college students who put on fifteen extra pounds during their freshman year. Wait until you turn forty. Whether there is scientific evidence to support such claims, researchers have found that some college students do indeed put on a few extra pounds their freshman and sophomore years. This is another reason to embrace walking on campus as much as possible. Exercise!

Depending on your class schedule, your homework, and if you have a job, exercising is probably the last thing on your mind. Your time is limited. Think of walking on campus as your exercise routine. Instead of jumping on the bus to take you across campus, consider leaving a few minutes earlier and walk to your class. If you have time between classes, take a short walk and explore the campus.

Because walking is so ingrained in your daily routine, many students don't think of it as "real" exercise. But it is. It will keep your blood pumping and your mind clear. Consider purchasing a pedometer. Track your mileage daily and see how it adds up. Regular walking:

✓ Burns calories
✓ Lowers cholesterol
✓ Lowers blood pressure
✓ Improves circulation
✓ Is easy on knees and other joints
✓ Increases cardiovascular endurance

Make certain you are prepared for rainy and winter months. In many parts of the country, the weather can become a real challenge. Have good boots for rain and snow. Be sure to have a decent umbrella and rain jacket. It may not be necessary to bring your ski gloves and scarf in August, but make sure they're available when the snow begins. You may not think it's necessary to have multiple pairs of shoes and sneakers. However, as sure as you are reading this, you will come back from class soaking wet one day.

If your campus receives a heavy snowfall or has an ice storm, use extra caution while walking. Avoid walking under trees as limbs could snap under the weight of the snow. Streets may not be thoroughly plowed and vehicles may not be able to stop. Be cautious while walking at night and make sure you're in well-lit areas.

Nearly all colleges and universities have campus escort services. They are wonderful services that should be fully utilized. Anytime you feel uneasy or unsafe, especially during evening hours, the campus escort service will walk with you or drive you anywhere on campus and to many locations off campus. Depending on your school, escort services may be available only at night; some are available 24-7. Check with your school as soon as you arrive on campus regarding the hours of operation, and always have the number with you.

You're also considered a pedestrian if you are roller blading. Most colleges and universities will allow roller blading on sidewalks. Be careful if this is your preferred mode of transportation. Students who are walking may not be alert when you come whizzing past them.

Pedal Power

If you're bringing a bike to campus, check with your school to see if bike registration is required. If your school doesn't require registration, I recommend that you register it anyway. Without proper registration, your bike will be almost impossible to recover if it's stolen. Provide the brand of your bike and serial number. If you're unable to locate a serial number, engrave your driver's license number on the frame (not your Social Security number!), and don't forget to take many photos.

Having a bike on campus can be very convenient; although you'll inevitably experience occasional frustrations, such as a flat tire, when you're running late for class. Most campuses will enforce the traffic laws regarding bicycles. You must comply with the same traffic laws as any other motorized vehicle, including stopping at all stop signs and red lights.

Riding a bike at night is not recommended. However, if you find that you may be doing so, make sure your bike is properly equipped. At minimum, reflectors should be installed on the front, back, and sides of the bike. Ideally, red-blinking strobe lamps should be installed on the back of the bike. A white light on the front of the bike is also recommended and can be purchased at most sporting goods stores. It's important to check your local laws. Some towns require bicycles to have lights that illuminate while riding at night.

It's recommended that you lock your bicycle only at approved bike racks. Most colleges have more than enough bike racks positioned throughout campus. Think twice about locking your bike to parking meters, signs, or trees. Many colleges and universities have ordinances against locking bikes on anything other than bike racks.

There are many bike locks from which to choose. U-locks, cable locks, and heavy chains are all popular. Although any locking device can be defeated if the crooks want your bike bad enough, heavy duty U-locks are apparently preferred. Always secure your locking device to the frame of the bike, not the tire. A few additional safety considerations are listed below.

✓ Wear a helmet.
✓ Don't wear flip-flops while riding a bike.

✓ Lock your bike every time. If you don't, it *will* be stolen. It makes no difference if it's a very expensive mountain bike or a bike under a hundred dollars. If it's unlocked, it will disappear.

✓ Lock your bike through the frame. If it's locked through the wheel, the tire can just be removed.

✓ When you leave school for a holiday, take extra time to secure your bike if you aren't taking it with you. If possible, put your bike in your room or lock it to a bike rack.

✓ When riding your bike on the road, ride on the right side, with the flow of traffic.

✓ Observe all traffic laws. Come to a complete stop at stop signs and traffic lights.

✓ Never talk on your cell phone while riding.

✓ Pedestrians have the right of way. If you come across people walking or riding their bike, warn them as you're passing by saying, "on your right," or "on your left."

✓ Use extra caution if you need to ride in the rain. Bike tires become very slippery, and cars also lose traction on wet pavement.

✓ When riding your bike, use caution when driving past parking lots. Drivers can't see the narrower profile of a bicycle or motorcycle.

Cars on Campus

Most of you heading to college have already been driving for a few years. I am sure you're quite skilled at driving around your hometown. However, navigating on a college campus, in an unfamiliar town with thousands of people milling in every direction, can present a new set of challenges.

College campuses can be very distracting. There can be so many students walking around it looks like bees buzzing a hive. First and foremost, always yield to a pedestrian. Yes, they may not be in the designated crosswalk area, and yes, you're running late for class, but that's no excuse for running someone over.

Before you leave for school with your set of wheels, take a few minutes to consider these suggestions for keeping you, your vehicle, and the public as safe as possible.

✓ Take your car to a mechanic. Have him thoroughly check it out. Get your brakes, headlights, taillights, and turn signals checked.

✓ Get a fresh oil change to begin the school year.

✓ Get new windshield wipers to begin the school year.

✓ Check all tires and make sure they are properly inflated.

✓ Have all the essentials, including proof of insurance and registration card.

✓ Carry a box or kit with the following items enclosed:
  ✓ Disposable camera
  ✓ Jumper cables
  ✓ Flares
  ✓ First aid kit
  ✓ Flashlight with good batteries
  ✓ Blanket
  ✓ Pen or pencil with a note pad

It's absolutely imperative that you notify your insurance company prior to departing for college. Depending on your carrier and where you'll be attending school, your rates may go up or down. Make sure you're completely covered in the event you're in an accident. Ask your agent about college discounts. Some insurance providers offer discounts to students who have recently graduated from high school with good grades. Additional discounts may apply if you maintain a certain grade point average in college. Also, ask your insurance agent if you're covered in the event you loan your vehicle to a friend and he happens to be in a collision.

If time permits, take your car and visit your campus before the school year begins. Get familiar with the entire campus. Find out where the closest gas station is located. Check out a possible mechanic. Better yet, look for two of them. Check out the parking facilities around campus and what part of the parking lot has the best lighting.

So the car is packed, and you're ready to rock and roll—head off to college, I mean. I trust you know you're about to become very popular. Yes, you have a great personality, and you are not too bad looking, but guess what? You have a set of wheels!

✎ **Hot Tip:**
A roadside assistance membership, like AAA, makes a great gift for students heading to college.

Other than the college quarterback, having a vehicle on campus puts you up with the top tier of popular college students. Congratulations. But prepare yourself—having a vehicle is a double-edged sword. There's no question having a vehicle can offer a great deal of flexibility, but it comes with a price. That price is additional responsibility and friends who can continually annoy you.

"Hey, Matt, do you mind buzzing me into town for a few minutes? I need to do a little grocery shopping." "Matt, it's raining really hard outside, can you drive me to the quad?" "Linda, if it's not too much trouble, can I hitch a ride with you when you go home? Just drop me off at the exit and my parents will pick me up." "By the way, Linda, are you driving back to campus on Sunday afternoon?"

Bumming rides is a way of life for students without cars. Don't fault the students though. For families with multiple children it can truly be a financial drain to have an extra vehicle in the family. In many ways, having a vehicle on campus can be a bonus. You're always in control. When you're in the dorms or living in an apartment, tell your friends that you'll happily drive them, but you do expect some help with gas money.

Having fellow students ride with you on long trips home can also have its advantages. With the price of fuel today, some students will actually advertise that they're leaving on a certain day and are willing to accept riders if the costs are shared. Most students are more than happy to split the gas money. If you have multiple riders sharing the costs, the trip becomes even less expensive. The extra students tagging along can also make for interesting conversation and thus make the ride seem shorter.

In any event, before deciding whether to bring a car to college or not, consider the following:

✔ Who is going to pay for the car repairs?

✔ Where's the best local mechanic?

✔ How far is the parking lot from your dormitory or apartment?

✔ What if the parking lot is full, can you go to other lots that are just as close?

✔ Do you know what to do if you lose your parking pass or permit?

✔ What do you do in the event you receive a ticket?

✔ It's the middle of winter and your car doesn't start, now what?

Developing good common sense habits from the moment you bring your car on campus can prevent many problems. For example, if you have an expensive stereo mounted in your car, consider getting a large towel, like a beach towel, and cover the entire dash area. Most criminals are not going to risk breaking in if they don't know what they're going to get. No matter where you drive or park on campus, there are a variety of precautions you should follow.

✔ Don't fumble around looking for your keys. Have them in your hand as you approach your car so you can get inside quickly and lock the door.

✔ Backing your car into a space is a good habit. It can give you better visibility and will allow you to pull out faster if necessary.

✔ As you pull into the parking lot, scan the area for someone who may be loitering.

✔ When parking your car in a parking lot, don't park near vans that have side doors that slide open.

✔ Don't announce to all your friends that you have your own car on campus.

✔ Always lock your vehicle, even if you leave it for a few minutes.

✔ Make sure you look inside your vehicle before getting in.

✔ Get in the habit of locking any belongings you have in the trunk. It may not be valuable to you, but it could be to someone else. Something inexpensive is not worth the hassle of a broken window.

✓ If you're driving and you pass a person who has a disabled vehicle on the side of the road, don't stop. Call 911 and notify the police about the situation.

✓ If you feel you're being followed, call the police but keep driving. Pull into a firehouse, police station, a convenience store, or anywhere the business is open.

✓ Never pick up a hitchhiker.

✓ In the event your car does breakdown, stay with the vehicle. Raise the hood, but get back in the car and lock the doors.

✓ Be selective where you park your vehicle.

✓ When parking your car on the street, turn your wheels tight against the curb. This makes it much more difficult for someone to tow your car.

✓ If driving at night and someone hits you or rear-ends you at a traffic light, wave or signal to them, but drive to a well-lit area. If they approach your car, keep all doors locked and just roll your window down a little bit. Women are often a target for this type of scheme.

✓ Try to avoid leaving your car unattended for an extended period of time in a parking lot.

✓ If you drive a minivan or a truck with vent windows, make sure they're tightly closed when you exit.

✓ Make sure you know your license plate number.

✓ If you're ever carjacked, give up your car and anything in it. Chances are someone brazen enough to commit a carjacking will be equally as bold to hurt you if you get in their way.

✓ Try not to use your cell phone while driving unless you have a hands-free device.

✓ NEVER text message while driving!

Anti-Theft Devices

Students are especially susceptible to car theft due to the number of cars on campus. Whether cars are old or new doesn't really matter. Don't think just because you have a ten-year-old Honda that it's not a target. It is!

Vehicles are stolen for a variety of reasons. For joy rides or for the parts or stereos or tires—with such a large selection of cars from which to choose, college campuses provide great opportunities for the car thief.

According to the National Insurance Crime Bureau, almost 1.2 million vehicles were stolen in 2006. Believe it or not, those numbers are slightly down compared to vehicle thefts in 2005. Every twenty-six seconds a motor vehicle is stolen in the United States.

Many vehicles purchased in the last few years come with a factory-installed anti-theft device or alarm system. These systems, either mechanical or electronic, are designed to deter your vehicle from being stolen.

Unfortunately, most of us have heard the annoying horn honking or siren wailing in the parking lot. Society has become desensitized to the noise. It's the car that cried wolf. Have you ever known anyone who has called the police because he heard a car alarm being activated? There has never been a total consensus if alarms actually reduce or deter car theft. You must know, if a professional car thief wants your car, he is going to steal it, alarm or not.

However, what about the thief who just wants a quick joy ride? The open parking lots of sprawling campuses make college students especially susceptible to auto theft. With many cars on campus from which to choose, the petty car thief may just pass on yours if it has an anti-theft device.

Alarms are meant to be a deterrent, not foolproof. Know this—most insurance companies will give you a discount if your vehicle does have an alarm system. You can choose from many models, which run anywhere from fifty dollars to more than a thousand, not including installation. Speak to your auto manufacturer or mechanic about which would be best for your vehicle. Determine your budget and whether an alarm is cost effective. For example, you may not want to install a $500 anti-theft device if your vehicle is only worth $1,500.

The National Insurance Crime Bureau, NICB, is the nation's leading not-for-profit organization dedicated exclusively to preventing, detecting, and defeating insurance fraud and vehicle theft through information analysis, investigations, training, and public awareness. They offer these suggestions to prevent your vehicle from being stolen, including a "layer" method of protection for high-risk vehicles.

LAYER #1—COMMON SENSE

✓ Ignition keys—Remove keys after every use.
✓ Lock doors and close windows.
✓ Park in a well-lit area.

LAYER #2—WARNING DEVICES

✓ Audible alarms—Equip with a motion- or impact-sensor and a 120-decibel siren.
✓ Steering column collars—Prevents thieves from hot-wiring the vehicle.
✓ Steering wheel locks—A metal bar designed to prevent the steering wheel from turning.
✓ Brake pedal lock—Prevents depression of the brake pedal.
✓ Wheel locks—Similar to the "boot" used by police departments.
✓ Tire deflators—Causes the tire to go flat if the tire rotates before device is removed.
✓ Theft deterrent decals—Visually warn thieves the vehicle is protected by an alarm.
✓ Identification markers—Security labels marking various vehicle parts.
✓ Window etching—Etching the vehicle windows with the VIN.
✓ Micro-dot marking—Spraying an epoxy resin on parts that can be traced back to vehicle.

LAYER #3—IMMOBILIZING DEVICES

✓ Smart keys—Keys containing computer chips. Without exact key, vehicle cannot be started.
✓ Fuse cut offs—Short-circuits the electrical system preventing vehicle from being started.
✓ Kill switches—Inhibits the flow of electricity or fuel to the engine by hidden switch.

✓ Starter, ignition, and fuel disablers—Causes vehicle to stop running in short time.

✓ Wireless ignition authentication—Transmitters that activate the ignition circuitry.

LAYER #4—TRACKING SYSTEMS

Systems emit a signal to police or a monitoring station when the vehicle is stolen, which allows the vehicle to be tracked.

Bus and Shuttle Services

Depending on the size of your school and its proximity to urban areas, you may have several choices regarding bus and shuttle services. Typically, your college will offer its own campus shuttle service, at no cost to you, which operates on a set schedule. Many campuses use a color-coded map to outline their route. It's important to know the shuttle schedule and hours of operation. Normally, they don't run twenty-four hours a day. Weekend schedules could also be modified. Additionally, most shuttle schedules will be curtailed on school breaks and holidays.

If your school is located near a major city, you may also have public bus transportation at your disposal. These services are a fare-based system; however, they will enable you to take advantage of reaching locations not serviced by your campus shuttle service. For example, many public bus transportation systems have routes from the campus to area shopping malls. Their schedule may also permit you to visit friends and family in neighboring towns. Once you arrive on campus, ask if your college is serviced by public transportation.

As the weather begins to deteriorate, buses will become crowded. Allow yourself extra time to make the bus and plan on a longer trip to campus. Many buses permit standing once the seats are full. Make sure you have an overhead stanchion to hold or a seat to lean against. Buses make sudden stops, and if you're not properly secured, you may be tossed around. Consider these other suggestions if you plan on traveling by bus.

✓ Never chase after a bus or pound on the side to get the driver's attention.

✓ Use caution when exiting the bus as the driver may have blind spots and be unable to see you.

✓ If you are traveling after dark, arrive at the bus stop just a minute or two before the bus is due. You may look vulnerable in the eyes of a criminal if you're standing for any length of time in the evening.

✓ Be careful at the bus stop. It's not uncommon for a large crowd to form while waiting at a popular stop. Make certain that you're not accidentally pushed into traffic by the crowd behind you as they begin to press their way onto the bus.

✓ If possible, sit near the driver.

✓ Be aware of who is around you and watch your belongings.

Living Off Campus

Whether you have a car, bicycle, or any other vehicle, much of the information discussed in this chapter will be modified if you are living off campus. In many respects, having a vehicle when living off campus can present a host of different and frustrating challenges.

More often than not, you'll still need to register your vehicle or bike even though you live off campus. Colleges will require you to have parking permits in order to park your car in one of the campus parking lots. Additionally, you may need a separate parking sticker to park on the street, near your house or apartment. If you have a bike, make sure that you bring it inside every night. If that's not practical, try to bring it on a porch and lock it to something secure.

Street parking can truly test the strength of your character. Every day when you pull out of your parking space, you may find your coveted spot taken upon return by another resident. You then must drive around the block numerous times in search of an open parking space. Once you find one, your adrenaline starts pumping with excitement until you realize that you're now further away from your apartment than your class was in the first place.

Winter weather is yet another ordeal. A snowstorm hits the evening before morning classes. It's freezing outside, and you would love to drive to campus. However, you already know that as soon as you pull out, someone is going to jump in your spot in the blink of an eye. Being the intellectual that you are, you get a few trashcans to set in your space after you leave. Hours later when you return from campus, you find your parking spot is no longer there, and the trash cans are thrown on the sidewalk. Since everyone else left their vehicles on the street, there are no other parking spaces to be found. You must drive back to campus, leave your car in the main parking lot, and walk back to your apartment.

Minor collisions can happen at any time. If you do have a fender-bender, make sure you pull well off the road before you exit your vehicle. If the collision is at night, drive to a populated area or call 911 and tell them you need assistance.

Heading Home for the Weekend

With the hustle and bustle of classes and studying, you may not have given your vehicle the maintenance attention it requires. Routine auto service can be difficult even for folks without your schedule. By following a few simple suggestions, you will lessen the probability of a breakdown and a delay in your travel plans.

- ✓ Before you depart, walk around the vehicle and make sure your tires are properly inflated.
- ✓ If your vehicle is known for leaking oil, double-check the oil level and carry an extra quart or two in the trunk.
- ✓ Make sure you check the tire pressure of the spare tire to ensure it is properly inflated. It may look full, but many times under the weight of the vehicle, it will go flat. If you don't have a tire pressure gauge, go to a local mechanic and request that the spare be checked.
- ✓ If you're traveling a long distance, try to obtain traveler's checks at your local bank instead of carrying a large amount of cash.
- ✓ If staying in a hotel, park in well-lit areas.
- ✓ Keep your hotel room key with you at all times and always have your door locked.

✓ Call your folks or the people you're visiting along the way. Tell them where you are on your route.

✓ If you are traveling in winter months, inclement weather may be a possibility. Make certain you have blankets, bottled water, and a few snacks.

✎ Hot Tip:
Carry a disposable camera in your glove box at all times.

A Staged Auto Accident

So you're driving down the street, minding your own business, and the driver in front of you slams on his brakes. You thought you were paying attention, but you end up hitting the rear end of his car. A normal everyday accident, right? Possibly, but you may have just been scammed!

According to Peter J. Johnson, Jr., president of the law firm Leahey & Johnson, and a legal analyst for *FOX News*, such accidents may be a scam: "Staged accidents . . . are quickly becoming one of the most common forms of insurance fraud in the United Sates. . . . I must tell you, in my daily law practice, it is one of the most disturbing things I see—accident fraud."

Johnson reported that the Insurance Research Council (IRC) estimated that 24 percent of auto injury claims may contain fraud or "build up," which can add approximately $4.5 billion annually to auto injury settlements. So what exactly is a staged accident? According to Peter Johnson, "A staged accident is an accident in which the participants (except you) are all involved in the accident and are part of the scam to defraud either you or an insurance company."

Johnson and *FOX News* featured three types of common road stings, as well as tips to help you avoid becoming a victim.

COMMON ROAD STINGS

✓ **The Drive Down.** These often take place at four-way stop signs, T-intersections, merge-and-yield signs, freeway ramps, and parking lots. You, the victim, attempt to merge your vehicle into traffic and another driver, the scammer, waves you forward. You say to yourself, "What a nice guy." But instead of letting you in, he speeds up his car and slams his car into yours. When the police show up, he of course denies that he ever motioned to you or waved you forward or indicates he was merely scratching his head or fixing something in the car.

✓ **The Panic Stop.** An old jalopy is filled with people ahead of you on the road. The scammer driving the old jalopy positions his car in front of yours while a back seat lookout in his vehicle waits for you to be distracted. Once he sees you're distracted, the scammer in front slams on the brakes and you rear-end the criminal's vehicle. You are shaken up and can't understand why the vehicle stopped so quickly. In order to provoke such accidents, staged accident rings will intentionally knock out brake-light bulbs so that there is no warning the vehicle is slowing down.

✓ **Swoop & Squat.** On a surface street, this scam usually involves three vehicles: two driven by the ring members and the other by you. The driver of the "squat" vehicle (full of passengers) puts his vehicle in front of yours, the second ring member driving the swoop vehicle pulls ahead of his comrade in crime and cuts it off causing the "squat" vehicle to hit his brakes. Obviously, you can't react in time and you rear-end the "squat" vehicle. Then incredibly, the "swoop" vehicle takes off from the scene never to be seen again. You, the innocent driver, play into the scam and blame the vehicle that took off—just as they had planned.

TIPS TO AVOID ACCIDENT SCAMS

✓ Pay attention and avoid tailgating. Allow plenty of space between your car and the car ahead of you if the car ahead suddenly decides to stop.

✓ Call the police and make a report even if the damage is minimal and everyone says they're okay and are feeling fine. Call 911 and insist on a report being taken to list the condition of the occupants and the damage to the vehicles.

✓ Be your own investigator. Carry a disposable camera to document the scene and damage to the vehicles and the identity of the people involved. Get as many names and phone numbers and driver's licenses as you can collect.

✓ Observe the physical condition and demeanor of everyone at the scene. Do they look hurt? What did they say after the accident?

✓ Report the accident to your insurance company. Don't be pennywise and pound foolish in failing to report the accident. If you don't report the accident and a claim is made, then you may not have coverage for the money damages that are being claimed against you.

✓ Beware of new friends. Understand that there are good Samaritans out there, but also know that the person who suddenly appears at the scene trying to direct you to certain attorneys or doctors may be part of the scam as well.

9

Living Off Campus

As students enter their junior and senior year, most will seek off-campus apartments. Occasionally, sophomores will move into an off-campus apartment, but most of the time, it's the upperclassmen.

Renting your first apartment has become a rite of passage. Similar to the dorms, off-campus apartment life can be a great deal of fun. Without question, it's a popular choice. But it also presents challenges. This chapter focuses on the precautions students must take to avoid becoming a victim of a crime or an accident.

The decision to move off campus should not be taken lightly. It's a newfound freedom that comes with its share of adult responsibilities and headaches. Many factors need to be considered. Apartment living is much different than living in the dorms as you will wear a variety of "hats." You'll be the security guard and the fire chief. You'll be the chef and the garbage man. You will bear a much greater responsibility for your overall safety and well-being than living in the dorms. Additionally, the financial implications of apartment living can affect you long after you graduate, if not handled properly.

Roommates

Really think about potential roommates. You may have a great friend you like to party with on the weekends, but do you really want to live with that person? What can you both afford? Are you paying the rent or will your parents pay? Are you and your parents going to split the costs? These questions are important because it may be in your best interest to include friends who have their parents' financial backing. The last thing you need is a roommate who's always tight on cash. The landlord doesn't care who gives him his rent; he just wants it, each month on time. Depending upon who signs the lease, you may end up responsible for your friend's share of the rent. If you're over eighteen, you're legally responsible for any agreements you enter.

Every one of us has special skills. Some will have habits that may be unappealing. Do you enjoy cooking? Is it going to be your responsibility to cook for everyone? Do your friends hate doing the laundry and keeping their room clean? You may think, "No big deal, it's their room." What will happen if every time you want to get a drink all the glasses are dirty and sitting in the sink? What will happen if you want to bring friends home to hang out and one of your roommates has clothes all over the apartment, not just in his room, but clothes laying everywhere?

Choosing your roommates wisely can save you a great deal of aggravation. Do any of your potential roommates smoke? Do you smoke and your roommates do not? If someone does smoke inside, understand that your house, furniture, and clothes will reek of smoke. Everyone has different expectations about living with other people. You must be honest with yourself. What if you have a friend who has great housekeeping qualities, but who loves loud head-banging music? How about someone who enjoys going to bed early, or likes staying up till 2 a.m. every night? Can you deal with those personality traits? Conflicts are bound to arise. However, keeping the lines of communication open is key to a successful roommate relationship.

What about your roommate's friends? Do they tend to socialize with known partiers? Are your friends aware that you are all responsible for each other's actions? Compatibility is more than just hanging out and having a few beers on the weekend.

Which Apartment to Choose?

Be certain to investigate many properties before signing a lease. Consider giving your parents the courtesy of reviewing your final selection prior to signing a lease. As you're researching apartments, look closely at the entire building. Make your decision on the complete house, not just one or two unique features. For example, you walk in and the family room is huge, complete with high ceilings and a large deck off the back door. The deck is definitely a plus, but the kitchen is tiny. In addition, the place can comfortably sleep four people, but there are only three bedrooms. Which of you wants to have another roommate? It could be a problem.

Before you sign a lease, however, first check with your college to see if they provide their own version of apartment housing. Many colleges and universities own properties off campus that are available for students to rent. In many cases, the university-owned properties are better maintained and equipped than individual landlord properties. Additionally, college towns are sure to have real-estate management companies handling multiple rental listings. These companies can make shopping for housing a tad easier as they usually have access to large inventories of apartments.

Apartments that are not under the control or supervision of campus officials should be scrutinized with a greater concern for safety. Safety standards that are present in dormitory living are curtailed or nonexistent in many off-campus apartments and houses. Yes, the buildings may technically meet the local codes in your area, but they may lack several safety essentials like sprinkler systems and hard-wired fire alarms.

When considering a location, take into account whether or not the apartment is near a campus bus service. Although you may have a vehicle, there will be times when you're unable to drive, like in bad weather or if your car breaks down. It's important to keep in mind that most off-street apartment parking is limited at best. When you leave for classes in the morning, it may be hard to find a parking space when you return. Considering the price of fuel, campus bus services may be the most economical mode of transportation as well.

Perhaps you check out an apartment, and it has all the features you're looking for, except it's much further off campus than you had desired. You don't have a problem with it because you have a car with a campus parking pass. Your roommates love it too, but they don't have a vehicle. Now what?

Can you really commit to driving them to campus everyday? Even in the freezing cold when you're not going to class? As you can see, living arrangements can become quite tricky.

It's paramount when shopping for an apartment that all of you are in attendance. Visit the apartment neighborhood during the weekday, as well as at night and on weekends. Despite conflicting schedules, be sure to find a time to view it with all potential roommates present. Walk through the house. Envision where your belongings will go. Does the apartment come furnished? Who is going to provide what furniture? Providing kitchen necessities and bathroom essentials can become rather expensive. Who will pay for them?

What about the bedrooms? In older buildings, they'll be different sizes. Who gets what room? These things must be worked out while you're all in attendance. The reason for hashing out the details prior to signing a lease is to prevent someone from moving out and sticking you with the rent. No doubt it's difficult to think about *getting stuck* when dealing with friends, but you'll need to protect yourself financially. Landlords can notify the credit bureaus and most will. Some landlords will pull credit reports on one or all of you before moving in. Additionally, some landlords will insist that your parents co-sign the lease.

When would you like to move into a new apartment? Ideally, you should give yourself two, three, or even four months to search for your new home. Even if the apartment you're visiting is already rented, you may be able to narrow the search to the section of town or neighborhood. If you wait too long, the inventory of available places will diminish, and you'll find yourself settling for less than you want. As you layout your wishlist for housing options, consider the following points as a guideline. They should be reviewed as you visit each home.

- ✓ How much money do you have to spend? What's your budget?
- ✓ Are utilities included? Gas, electric, heat, water, sewage, garbage, cable, lawn maintenance, etc.
- ✓ What type of security deposit is required?
- ✓ Does the landlord require a co-signer?

✔ What's the term of the lease? How long is it for?

✔ Where is the closest laundry facility?

✔ Would you prefer that you are still able to walk to campus and your classes?

✔ Do you have an Internet connection? Internet service is a must. Will you have access to high speed or dial up. Will your roommates split the cost of Internet service?

✔ Are pets allowed?

✔ Is there ample parking for cars?

✔ Are the parking areas well lit?

✔ Is there a place inside to put your bike?

✔ Is a bus stop nearby?

✔ Is a grocery store close?

✔ Does the campus shuttle bus have a route in this direction?

✔ Is the apartment fully furnished?

✔ Does it have air conditioning?

✔ Are there screens in the windows? Are they in decent shape?

✔ When was the last time the place was painted?

✔ What's the condition of the bathrooms and how many are there?

✔ Are you allowed to use a grill on the premises?

✔ Make sure you and your roommates understand everything in the lease. It is a legally binding document.

Student Renter's Responsibilities

As a tenant and leaseholder, your responsibility goes far beyond living in the dorms. You are contractually bound, along with your roommates, to fulfill the landlord's lease—so read the lease carefully. If you violate the terms and default on the lease, your landlord can file a claim and take you to court. Additionally, he can hold anyone who signed the lease legally responsible for any money that is owed or any damage that was done to the property. The landlord can also notify the credit bureaus of the breach of contract. Believe me, the landlord has no desire to engage in any legal battle. It's rather simple; the landlord wants to be paid, and he does not want his property trashed. That being said, most leases will feature standard clauses that will require you to:

✔ Pay the rent on time. This doesn't mean just *your share* of the rent. You may be liable for your roommate's financial portion as well if your roommate fails to pay his or her share.

✔ Pay the utilities on time, if not included in the rent.

✔ Maintain the property in a clean and safe manner.

✔ Notify the landlord if the property is damaged.

✔ Give your landlord access to the property with reasonable notification and during an emergency.

✔ Limit the amount of people living in the building. Most rental properties have a maximum occupancy capacity.

✔ Provide written notification of your intent to terminate the lease. The use of certified mail may be required.

✔ Get permission to own pets, and often this is strictly limited with some obvious exceptions, such as seeing-eye dogs.

✔ Leave the apartment clean and undamaged upon moving out, if you want to have your security deposit returned.

A lease will often prohibit you from the following without permission:

✔ Making repairs or alterations to the property.

✔ Changing the locks.

✔ Subletting the apartment.

Landlord Responsibilities

Conversely, the landlord has responsibilities to *you*, too. He must maintain the property in accordance with local and state building codes. He must provide a safe and secure building environment for you to reside. He must respond to your questions and concerns within a reasonable amount of time. You are strongly urged to have your parents review the lease to ensure that the lease is consistent with typical landlord-tenant responsibilities.

Items to consider:

✔ Are there enough smoke alarms in the apartment?

✔ Is there a smoke alarm on each floor?

✔ Are they hard-wired, or do they require batteries?

✔ Are the smoke alarms wired together?

✔ Are there carbon monoxide detectors installed?

✔ Install a carbon monoxide detector yourself, even if there is no gas stove. Effective January 1, 2007, every Illinois home is required to have a carbon monoxide detector within fifteen feet of any room used for sleeping. Apartments with several floors and separate bedrooms will need multiple carbon monoxide detectors.

✔ Would the landlord install deadbolts if they are not in place, or would he mind if you installed them? If you facilitate the installation of the locks, ask the landlord if the cost of the locks can be deducted off your first month's rent.

✔ Ask the landlord to install a peep hole in your door so you can view people outside without opening the door?

✔ Make sure your lease stipulates who is responsible for repairs. ·

✔ The landlord should make repairs and address your concerns in a timely manner.

✔ Make certain the landlord is responsible for maintaining the exterior of the building, including pruning bushes and trees.

✔ The landlord should respect your privacy at all times.

✔ The landlord retains the right to terminate the lease should you violate the terms and conditions.

✔ The landlord should not delay refunding your security deposit once conditions are met.

Carbon Monoxide Detectors

Seldom do students consider moving into an apartment without having at least one working fire alarm. Actually, any time a building is used for rental purposes, fire alarms are required under the law. Depending on the local ordinance of the town where you reside, multiple fire alarms may be mandatory.

Often overlooked, however, but equally important, are carbon monoxide detectors, or CO2 alarms. There is a good chance that the apartment you're renting does not have a CO2 alarm installed. Quite possibly, your parents may not have a CO2 alarm installed in their house either. Because carbon monoxide detectors are not required under the law in all fifty states, they tend to be ignored.

Every year more than 500 people die from carbon monoxide poisoning, and thousands more are taken to the hospital. Your vehicles, hot water heaters, gas stoves, and gas furnaces all produce deadly carbon monoxide emissions. CO2 is also produced by other sources such as wood-burning stoves, gas-powered tools, and propane camping stoves, just to name a few.

On August 19th, 2007, one day before the fall semester was to begin at Virginia Tech, the university was jolted once again by an emergency. Hours before a memorial was to be dedicated in honor of the students and faculty members who were killed on campus in April 2007, more than twenty students were rushed to the hospital with carbon monoxide poisoning.

Students renting an off-campus apartment were poisoned because of a faulty water-heater valve. As the gas company and fire personnel arrived at the apartment complex, lethal levels of carbon monoxide were detected throughout the structure. There were no carbon monoxide detectors anywhere in the multi-unit apartment building.

Fortunately, everyone survived this incident, which is something of a miracle. Five of the girls were unconscious for a number of days. Thankfully, they don't appear to have suffered any permanent injuries, but doctors continue to monitor their health for lingering effects.

WHAT TO DO IN A CO2 EMERGENCY

Carbon monoxide is a colorless, odorless, tasteless gas that is very difficult to detect. It is a highly toxic gas that can kill in a short amount of time if not detected. Carbon monoxide poisoning can cause the following symptoms:

✓ Nausea
✓ Dizziness

✓ Headaches
✓ Flu-like symptoms
✓ Shortness of breath

If you believe you have been exposed to CO2 gas, it is imperative to get outside and into fresh air immediately! Call the police and fire department without delay. If you come across people you believe have been overcome by carbon monoxide, get them outside at once. If they are unconscious and you're unable to get them out of the house, open all doors, windows, and garages and try to ventilate the area. If you are able to safely move about the premises, shut down all combustion appliances, such as the water heater, gas stove, and furnace.

Carbon monoxide detectors can be purchased at any home improvement stores. They range in price from $15 to $50. Ideally, they should be installed in the hallway directly outside of your bedroom and other sleeping areas. Ask your landlord if you purchase a CO2 detector for the apartment, would he consider taking the price of the unit off the first month's rent. If you don't have the money to purchase one, call home and ask your parents to buy a CO2 alarm for you.

A Roommate Contract

"Roommate contracts" are becoming more popular with students. These contracts are designed to provide basic guidelines about your new living arrangements. Roommate contracts outline who does what and who pays for what. Nothing is worse than moving into your new apartment and having a roommate say, "I never said I was going to do that." Drafting such a contract may seem "cold," but it's a move that can prevent problems as the school year goes on.

Sharing items can also cause problems. Will everything be shared equally? How will utilities be divided, and who will be responsible for collecting the money? Are you allowed to use each other's computers? What about food? Who does the grocery shopping? Are you all individually responsible for buying your own food? Will the food you purchased be shared? Potential roommates can avoid disagreements by simply stipulating, in advance, the ground rules for living together. Other issues to contend with in a roommate contract are attitudes towards parties, alcohol, drugs, and overnight guests. How will you feel if your roommate's girlfriend is sleeping over every weekend? Being as honest as possible will help to create the harmony that's essential to successful apartment living.

In addition to defining the above responsibilities, small household supplies that appear insignificant can become costly month in and month out. It may benefit you to define who will pay for the following items:

✓ Trash bags
✓ Cleaning supplies
✓ Paper towels
✓ Bath soap
✓ Vacuum bags
✓ Dish detergent
✓ Paper products
✓ Toilet paper
✓ Shampoo and conditioner
✓ Toner cartridges and computer paper

Safety

Whatever apartment you do finally decide to rent, security and safety should top the priority list of concerns. Most importantly, do not make your apartment an easy target. Because you and your roommates are now completely responsible for your well-being, it's important to take precautions to prevent injuries, crimes, and accidents.

✓ Keep your doors and windows locked when you're not home. Remember, there is no front desk and no security. You are the security guard.
✓ Always double-check the windows and doors when you're leaving or going to bed. It's a good habit to get into.
✓ Don't display any valuables in your window, like televisions, com-

puters, and other electronics such as iPods. If having these items near windows is your only option, ask the landlord if you're able to install drapes or curtains.

✓ Make sure curtains are drawn when you're at class or gone for the day. Don't let outsiders know your routine.

✓ Use caution when setting up your voice mail or answering machine. Be very vague with your outgoing message so people don't know your schedule. It's better to say something like, "Thanks for calling. We can't take your call right now. Please leave a message, and we'll call you back." Versus, "Cheryl and I are out. We're either at class or out on the town, we'll be home by 7 p.m. Leave us a message and one of us will call you back."

✓ Make sure the exterior of your apartment is well lit. Ask your land-lord who is responsible for exterior lighting.

✓ Don't give out duplicates of your keys; keep your keys with you at all times.

✓ If you are home alone, turn on a few extra lights to give the appear-ance you're not alone.

✓ Never put your full name on your mailbox or door. Use the first initial and your full last name.

✓ Never keep keys under doormats, in the mail box, or above the door. Pin an extra one in your backpack, but don't label it.

✓ Double-check that all appliances are turned off before you leave for the day.

✓ Ask the landlord if he installed new locks prior to moving in. If he tells you that the prior tenants returned all the keys, ask him if he knows for sure that copies weren't made.

✓ Make sure your new house has a few flashlights with good batteries. Sooner or later a storm will come through and knock out your power. If the power is out for a long period of time, notify your landlord. If power goes out in the winter, immediately let your landlord know.

✓ Don't overlook simple things like clearing the snow and ice off steps and sidewalks. Find out if that is your responsibility or your land-lords.

✔ It's rare, but occasionally an off-campus house may include a garage. Typically these garages are older in nature and positioned in the back of the house or located off an alley. Use caution if you decide to store anything in these garages.

✔ Require your landlord to give you advanced notice if he intends to work on the property. Also tell him you would prefer to be home while the maintenance is being completed.

✔ If you ever drop your car off to be repaired, make sure they only get your car keys. Keep your apartment key on a separate ring.

✔ Get to know your neighbors. They can prove to be a great ally.

✔ If you must use laundry facilities in town, try to do laundry during the day. If that's not possible because of class schedules, wait until someone can go with you.

✔ If you arrive home, and you think things are out of place, step back out of the house and call 911 immediately.

Figuratively speaking, when you sign a lease that property is yours. Some landlords are more particular than others. However, all would expect you to uphold a basic level of maintenance and upkeep. Pick up any garbage around the house. Make small repairs when necessary. Remember to take your trash cans in on trash day. Don't call the landlord if you stop-up the toilet. Buy a plunger. Although much of the outside may not be your responsibility, take some pride in your house. If you see a large weed you don't need to wait for the landlord, yank it out yourself. I know, I know you're paying a lot for the place. Just remember, when you move out the landlord has your security deposit. By cementing a good relationship with your landlord and maintaining the property, you are ensuring the return of your security deposit.

A Party in Your New Apartment

Now we're talking! You and your roommates are finally moved in, and it's time to celebrate. Before you do anything though, sit down with everyone and plan this thing out. I know you're excited, but having half the campus show up at your front door can put a damper on things real fast, especially when two guys wearing blue uniforms and badges walk in.

It may be difficult, but consider keeping your first gig low profile. I realize you may want to invite everyone you know, particularly your old friends in the dorm, friends from your sports team, the kids in your economics class, and the girls. Oh man, you almost forgot the girls! Parties off campus have a habit of taking on a life of their own. The phrase "open party" can spread around campus faster than a forest fire on a hot summer day. No question those types of parties make for great stories later in life, but let someone else be the host. The additional cost and the damage they cause are not worth the headache. Exercise restraint with your guest list.

It's important to remember that you and your roommates are responsible for the safety and well-being of your guests. Additionally, you may be held liable for their behavior in and out of the house. I know you would never think of this, but remember how your friends tried to get served when they were underage? Well, don't think that has changed just because you have an apartment. Underage students will seek out your party if they know alcohol is readily available. The last thing in the world you need is a guest getting hurt after you served them alcohol.

It may sound odd, but notify all your neighbors that you're having a get-together. Ask them to talk to you first if they have a problem with anything. That may help to avert any big confrontations. A few other suggestions are listed below.

- ✓ Write out a guest list. Have someone at the door crossing off names as guests arrive. Anyone not on the list should at least give you a name of someone they know. If someone unknown comes to the door, simply say, "I'm sorry, it's a closed party." Don't let anyone in your house you don't know.
- ✓ Keep the party inside. Don't let your guests spill into your neighbor's yard or on the street.
- ✓ Keep an eye on where your guests parked their cars. Don't allow them to block-in your neighbors.
- ✓ Make certain anyone drinking alcohol is of legal age.
- ✓ Not everyone wants to drink alcohol. Have an alternative available.

✓ Observe the amount of alcohol guests are consuming.

✓ Serve foods that aren't salty. They just promote drinking.

✓ See to it that guests aren't using the outside as a restroom.

✓ Never allow someone to leave and drive under the influence. Drive them home if you must.

✓ Never let anyone leave with an open container of alcohol from your house.

✓ Consider making bottled water available midway through the party. You'll be surprised how many guests grab a bottle.

✓ After the party, walk through the entire house. Make sure no one is left behind in your bedrooms, closets, or bathrooms. Check couches and furniture for smoldering cigarettes.

✓ Walk the entire perimeter of your house and pick up any garbage.

Make it a point to get to know your neighbors. They will probably want to meet you as well. It's very important to treat your neighbors with the same respect you would expect. Your next-door neighbor may become your biggest fan or your worst nightmare. Take the initiative to become friends.

So, You Think You Can Cook?

Okay, so you have a few culinary skills. But just because you threw burgers on the campfire while you were camping this past summer doesn't make you Emeril Lagasse. I know you can make a mean mac and cheese, and your spaghetti and Ragu is out of this world, but I'm trying to keep you safe here, not write *Tom's College Kitchen Cookbook*.

Let's talk burgers. Say you have a hankering for one of your famous half-pound monsters. Since you were a little tight on cash when you went to the grocery store, you were more focused on the total bill than the fat content of the ground chuck. I understand. But instead of purchasing a nice lean 90 percent to 10 percent mix (90 percent being the amount of beef and 10 percent being the amount of fat), you opted for the 70/30 he-man ratio because it was only two bucks for five pounds. A bargain for sure.

When you arrive home, your two roommates have the munchies as well, so they ask you to toss one on for them. Since you're not allowed to grill outside, you pull out the fry pan and pour just a little oil in the pan. I mean you don't want them to stick. Being the chef you are, you put the ground beef in a bowl, throw on your famous secret sauce and crack in an egg. Your roommates are now thoroughly impressed with the egg trick. As the pan starts sizzling you begin to form five burgers, at least a half-pound each. Your roommates are pulling out the paper plates and condiments as you drop those babies in the pan. You shout out a resounding, "Yikes!" as hot oil splatters on your arms.

You're all set. The burgers are snapping away in the pan, and it's time to flip them. With spatula at the ready, you flip those suckers over, but there's a half inch of grease in the bottom of the pan. As you flip your second burger, grease spills out of the pan and directly on top of the stove. Almost instantly, you have two-foot flames shooting over the pan. You have a great grease fire going! Do you know what to do? No, don't try to save the burgers! As you and your roommates are shouting a few expletives, try some of these suggestions:

- ✓ Put a lid on top of the pan. This should suffocate the fire.
- ✓ Turn off the stove.
- ✓ Call 911 if the first few attempts fail to put out the fire.
- ✓ Put a large amount of baking soda on the fire.
- ✓ Never use water to put out a grease fire; it will spread.
- ✓ Never use flour or baking powder.
- ✓ Don't hesitate to use the fire extinguisher that's supposed to be in your kitchen. Make sure it's rated for grease fires.
- ✓ Never try to carry the pan outside while it's still flaming.

Unforeseen things happen in the kitchen all the time. If you have a fire in the oven, shut the door, and turn off the oven. The same holds true for a microwave fire. Shut the door and unplug the microwave. If for any reason, the fire is not going out, call 911 immediately. It's better to error on the side of caution and have the fire department on its way.

Other cooking tips:

✔ Never leave cooking food unattended.

✔ Keep your stove top and oven clean at all times.

✔ Keep pot handles turned away from the edge.

✔ Watch for steam when using the microwave.

✔ Cooking popcorn in the microwave can burn you.

✔ Watch out for loose clothing or long-sleeved shirts.

✔ Make sure you have pot holders or oven mitts in the kitchen.

✔ Only clean the surface of the stove after it has completely cooled.

✔ If you are allowed to use a gas or charcoal grill, make sure it is placed far enough from the house.

✔ Use caution with propane tanks.

✔ Never use gasoline to start a grill.

✔ Never add extra lighter fluid because you think the coals aren't hot enough.

✔ Let the lighter fluid burn off before putting on the meat. If not, your burgers will taste like lighter fluid.

✔ If you get a grease fire in your grill, put the lid on tightly.

✔ Keep a fire extinguisher handy, even if you're cooking outside.

Unfortunately, off-campus apartment fires are not uncommon. According to the Center for Campus Fire Safety, between January 2000 and December 15, 2006, there were ninety-four fire fatalities in student housing. Almost 80 percent of those deaths have occurred in off-campus housing such as rented houses and apartments. The Center for Campus Fire Safety cites these common factors in a number of fires.

1. Lack of automatic fire sprinklers.
2. Missing or disabled smoke alarms.
3. Careless disposal of smoking materials.
4. Alcohol consumption.

The Center for Campus Fire Safety is a wonderful nonprofit organization "devoted to reducing the loss of life from fire at our nation's campuses." Check them out at www.campusfire.org.

Off-campus fires have other common denominators. Some apartments and Greek housing are older and, therefore, have wiring that doesn't conform to current safety code regulations, or students overload systems with the amount of electronic equipment they have today. Students cooking in their own kitchens may be inexperienced. Many older buildings lack working smoke alarms, sprinkler systems, and escape routes. Combine that with students who smoke or leave candles unattended, and it makes for an unsafe situation. Fires can occur at anytime and in any apartment. Consider these fire-safety precautions when you rent your next apartment.

✓ Smoke alarm batteries should be changed at the beginning of each semester. Never take out batteries in a smoke alarm that is beeping intermittently with the thought, "I'll replace those tomorrow." Have extra batteries available.

✓ Apartment buildings may have just enough smoke alarms to pass the local fire code. Make sure or purchase a UL-listed fire alarm and put one on every floor.

✓ If you're on a higher floor of an apartment, and there are limited escape routes, purchase a "fire-escape ladder" at a home improvement store for each bedroom.

✓ You must have more than one escape route in your apartment or off-campus house.

✓ If you have a party, walk around the house and make sure your friends didn't leave a cigarette lit in an ashtray or smoldering in a cup.

✓ Use extra caution not to overload apartment electrical outlets.

✓ If your apartment is on fire and you see smoke and flames, use a window to escape. If you don't have an escape ladder, tie bed sheets or clothes together to lessen your fall. A broken leg is much better than trying to get through smoke and flames.

✓ It's important that you and your friends keep your apartment in good housekeeping order. I realize that may be a lot to ask, but excessive clothes, books, magazines, and papers provide a great source of fuel for fires.

✓ If your apartment has a basement, use caution when near the wiring. Don't stack boxes throughout the basement.

✓ If you have your own laundry room in your apartment, regularly check the dryer for lint. It's also very important to clean out the dryer hose leading outside the building.

✓ Make sure there are working fire extinguishers that have been properly inspected with current dates. Also, make sure the fire extinguishers are large enough and rated for different fires.

✓ Never use a kerosene heater in an apartment or house.

Securing Your Apartment While on Break

So it's time to go home for a well-deserved break. Whether you'll be gone for a few weeks over Christmas or just heading home over the weekend for a home-cooked meal, there are a few things you should do to secure your apartment before you leave.

✓ Don't change your outgoing voice mail message to announce that you're out of town.

✓ Don't advertise that you are leaving for any length of time.

✓ Make sure someone is picking up the mail and newspapers or have them stopped while you're away.

✓ If you're responsible for your lawn, make sure it's mowed prior to leaving.

✓ Buy timers—they're cheap and are a wonderful deterrent. Buy at least two timers, one for downstairs and one for upstairs. Having the television or radio come on and lights set at different intervals while you're gone can be helpful in fooling an opportunistic criminal looking for a "sure thing." Set your downstairs' timers to come on just as it begins to get dark. Time them to go off when you would normally go to sleep. Set the upstairs' timer about an hour before you would go to bed and leave it on for about an hour after you would normally go to sleep. (Make sure nothing flammable is near an unattended light. Never drape fabric over a light for "atmosphere.")

✓ Tell a trusted neighbor or friend what your weekend or vacation schedule is going to be. Consider giving them a phone number where you can be reached.

✓ Consider shutting off your water if you have access to the shut-off valve. At minimum, double-check that faucets and toilets are not running when you leave.

✓ In the winter, you can turn the heat down when you're not home, but it's not advisable to turn the heat off completely—water in the pipes may freeze and burst.

✓ Take any valuables with you.

✓ Be certain all doors and windows are locked tight.

✓ If you have a sliding glass door in your apartment, make sure you have a piece of wood that can be placed in the track to prevent the door from opening.

✓ Close any blinds and drapes.

✓ Consider notifying police and ask them to keep a watch on your place. Police will often make an extra effort to patrol by your house.

Renter's Insurance

A 2006 Insurance Research Council poll found that 96 percent of homeowners had insurance while only 43 percent of renters had insurance. Many students are under the impression they don't need renter's insurance because they'll be covered under their landlord's policy. This is not correct. You may still be under your parent's policy, but not your landlord's. More than likely, your landlord's policy only covers the building you will be renting. Your landlord's policy will not cover your belongings or your liability. Read your lease carefully. It may require you to have renter's insurance, including liability coverage.

It's imperative that you check with your parent's insurance prior to signing a lease. Find out exactly what is covered and what is not. "A good rule of thumb for parents and students to gauge this is to examine to what extent the student is still a dependent," says Jeff McCollum, spokesperson for State Farm insurance.

Some items may not be covered under a typical renter's policy. "That is why parents and students might want to consider a 'personal articles policy.' These are very, very inexpensive policies that cover particular high-ticket or hard-to-replace items," says McCollum.

It's also very important to have liability insurance. Sadly, we live in an era where folks litigate every chance they can. Sooner or later, you and your roommates will have a party. Chances are alcohol will be present. If someone gets injured at your party, you could be held liable. Also, you may not think your belongings are worth that much. However, if you had to replace them today, what would the cost be?

 Hot Tip:
Whatever you do, purchase renter's insurance!

10

The World Is Just a Click Away

The tech-savvy world in which we live today was not a concern for the average college student years ago. Throughout most of the 1980s, students were still typing reports on typewriters, and research was done only in the library. For those who were in school before the 1980s, the only computer was the size of two cars located in a room bigger than the average house.

When most of your parents went to college, they were fortunate if they owned a Smith Corona typewriter. If their typewriter was electric, with a double ribbon and reverse key, they were living large. Today, we have unimaginable technology at our fingertips. With chat rooms, iPods, BlackBerrys, cell phone cameras, text messaging, laptops with wireless cards, Nintendo Wii, and Xbox 360 so entrenched in our daily lives, it's no wonder I can't get anyone to play Monopoly. Come on, one quick game. I'll be the "hat."

Yes, some things *have* changed since your parents went to school. Over the past fifteen to twenty years, technology has evolved at lightning speed. Almost every home in America has a computer. Children in kindergarten have access to computers in their classrooms. High school and college students do a large percentage of their work on personal computers. Businesses have come to rely on computers so much that our economy would be significantly altered if companies operated on 1980's technology.

Computers and the Internet are a vital part of our lives, and they're here to stay. As with anything so advanced and helpful, there's sure to be a downside. We've come to rely on computers so much, that the tiniest of glitches can wreak havoc on our day. If the computer crashes in the middle of a term paper or the Internet goes down for two hours, panic sets in. When you factor in computer viruses, Internet predators, identity thieves, and potential employers searching your online profile, you begin to understand why security measures and precautions must be considered.

The Equipment

Before you begin to pack the family minivan and head off to college, let's first take a look at the various pieces of computer equipment that you may bring along. As far as the computer itself, you will have to choose between a desktop and a laptop. Each one has its pluses and minuses, so it really comes down to your personal preference. Clearly, a desktop system is bigger and more cumbersome than a laptop, but it also makes it more difficult to steal. Between the heavy CPU and separate monitor, stealing a desktop is not the first choice among computer thieves.

A laptop, however, is an ideal prize for any thief. They are expensive, portable, and easy to resell. In addition to your computer, more than likely you will have a printer with extra cartridges of ink. Whether you prefer a desk-jet or laser printer, both are lightweight and easily stolen. Almost as expensive as the printer are the ink cartridges. Most students beginning a new school year are stocked up with both black and color cartridges. Although printer specific, with an average price of $30 dollars per cartridge, these little packages can be effortlessly stolen, and they are untraceable.

There is also a good chance that you will have a few surge protectors, CDs, extra USB cables, and maybe an external hard drive or back-up system. Your equipment must be secured. Thieves know that students often neglect to secure their belongings, so it's important to beat them at their own game and take precautions both before you leave for school and on campus.

✓ Speak with your insurance agent *before* you leave for school and give him or her a list of everything you are taking. Make certain all of your computer equipment is covered in the event of a theft or an accident.

✓ Write down all serial numbers, model numbers, and prices paid for your equipment. Keep all receipts if possible.

✓ Consider engraving all of your equipment with your driver's license number. You should be able to sign out an engraver's tool from campus security.

✓ At a minimum, put a mark or apply an indelible label with your contact information on every piece of electronic equipment. Thieves will move on if they see a label that is difficult to remove.

✓ Take photos of all your equipment. Keep a set at home and bring a set of photos with you to school.

✓ Keep all extra computer supplies like ink, cables, and CDs locked in your desk or closet at all times. They are easily stolen if left in the open.

✓ Never walk away or leave your laptop unattended, whether in your dorm, library, or local coffeehouse; it will be stolen if left unsecured. Take it to the restroom if nobody is able to watch it for you.

Just Plug It in and Go

You certainly can, but it may not be the safest course of action. Now that you're unpacked and the computer equipment is secured, it's time to talk about securing your work and yourself. Undoubtedly, you'll have a significant amount of schoolwork, if not all of it, on your computer. Even though insurance may be able to replace your laptop, the information stored on your computer is not easily recaptured. Nothing could be worse than taking a semester of notes and writing papers and having your computer crash or be stolen.

Whether you're a tech-wizard or not, you must also consider steps to keep yourself and your personal information protected. Campus computer networks are not entirely failsafe. Students can download superfluous information, and identity thieves may have the knowledge to tap into your system. From computer viruses and hackers to spam and spyware, it's vitally important that you create a defense to fight against potential hazards. Listed below are suggestions to help shield you from many computer-related troubles.

- ✓ Backup your information every few days. Use a CD, an external hard drive, a flash drive, or e-mail your notes and papers to a separate online server. Backing up your information must become a habit.
- ✓ Never share your password with anyone. If someone has your password, they have access to your computer at any time.
- ✓ Change your password regularly.
- ✓ Many Internet service providers or ISPs allow you to have several different e-mail addresses. Set up multiple screen names or e-mail accounts.
- ✓ Don't open any e-mails or instant messages from senders whose name you don't recognize. Be on the alert for "tricks" and seductive subject lines enticing you to open infected e-mails and files.
- ✓ Install antivirus software, a spam filter, and personal firewalls to prevent against a barrage of annoying adware and spyware pop-ups, as well as unauthorized people attempting to access your information.
- ✓ Use caution when sharing files and answering e-mails from unknown people. You may get a computer virus by simply opening up a file.
- ✓ Be careful when using public wireless networks, especially if you'll be entering your credit card number. Hackers and cyber-criminals can get around many public security systems.

Social Networking Websites

Social networking sites such as MySpace and Facebook are a relatively new phenomenon, but they're already totally entrenched in college life. With hundreds of sites from which to choose, social networking websites connect people with shared interests. You can interact using a variety of online methods, including e-mail, instant messaging, blogging, file sharing, discussion groups, and voice chatting.

Two of the most popular sites, MySpace and Facebook, have hundreds of millions of users and visitors, and can register hundreds of thousands of new users per day. Similar to other forms of new technology, MySpace and Facebook have their advantages and disadvantages. On one hand, these sites enable students to freely express themselves and communicate with friends. On the other hand, students have been expelled from school, fired from jobs, or rejected for a job because of the things they have posted on those sites.

While there's no denying the phenomenal success that MySpace and Facebook have enjoyed, students are lulled into a false sense of security due to the perceived anonymity of the website's security preferences. Because of that misperception, students tend to let their guard down and will post information that may become problematic later in life. I like to call this the Boomerang Effect—sooner or later it may come right back and hit you squarely in the head.

MySpace and Facebook are extremely clear in their privacy policies about what they can and cannot protect. However, students don't fully understand that there may be inherent risks with posting questionable information. If you choose to have a profile on *any* social networking website, it's imperative that you read the sites privacy policy in detail. Most students I've interviewed said they never bothered to read the policy.

AN EXCERPT FROM FACEBOOK'S PRIVACY POLICY

Facebook's privacy policy is very thorough and broken down into subcategories. One section of the policy is titled, "The Information We Collect." Within that section is the following:

> You post User Content (as defined in the Facebook Terms of Use) on the Site at your risk. Although we allow you to set privacy options that limit access to your pages, please be aware that no security measures are perfect or impenetrable. We cannot control the actions of the other Users with whom you may choose to share your pages and information. Therefore, we cannot and do not guarantee that User Content

you post on the Site will not be viewed by unauthorized persons. We are not responsible for circumvention of any privacy settings or security measures contained on the Site. You understand and acknowledge that, even after removal, copies of User Content may remain viewable in cached and archived pages or if other Users have copied or stored your User Content.

AN EXCERPT FROM FACEBOOK: SHARING YOUR INFORMATION WITH THIRD PARTIES

When you use Facebook, certain information you post or share with third parties (e.g., a friend or someone in your network), such as personal information, comments, messages, photos, videos, marketplace listings, or other information, may be shared with other users in accordance with the privacy settings you select. All such sharing of information is done at your own risk. Please keep in mind that if you disclose personal information in your profile or when posting comments, messages, photos, videos, marketplace listings or other items, this information may become publicly available.

MYSPACE PRIVACY POLICY

Similar to Facebook, MySpace has a highly detailed privacy policy as well. Under the heading "security," MySpace writes the following:

MySpace.com member accounts are secured by member-created passwords. MySpace.com takes precautions to insure that member account information is kept private. We use reasonable measures to protect member information that is stored within our database, and we restrict access to member information to those employees who need access to perform their job functions, such as our customer service personnel and technical staff. Please note that we cannot guarantee the security of member account information. Unauthorized entry or use, hardware or software failure, and other factors may compromise the security of member information at any time. For additional information about the security measures we use on MySpace.com, please contact us at privacy@myspace.com.

In the summer of 2007, officials at MySpace found more than 29,000 registered sex offenders with profiles on the website. Although MySpace did identify and remove the sex offenders from the site, there's no way MySpace or Facebook can prevent sex offenders from having profiles. Under the current set up requirements for both sites, users are not required to authenticate their identity.

Although 29,000 sex offenders were confirmed on MySpace, the possibility remains that hundreds of thousands of sex offenders could have profiles using pseudonyms. Even if laws are passed that require users to validate their identity, it will prove totally futile. It's completely unrealistic to monitor website activity with hundreds of millions of users. Also, since it's not feasible to observe the user at the other end of the keyboard, passing legislation that requires a user to confirm his identity is completely unworkable. The bottom line is you will never know for certain with whom you are chatting or who has your information. Knowing this, the responsibility for personal protection falls directly on you, the end-user.

It's important to note that there is nothing inherently wrong or dangerous with Facebook, MySpace, or other similar social networking websites. The risks involved are primarily user miscalculations regarding posting personal information under the guise of privacy. However, you can certainly enjoy yourself on these sites without compromising your security and reputation, not only while you are in school, but also long after you graduate.

Students can easily get caught up in the moment of a fun evening or an event and post information that they later regret. I'm certainly not suggesting that you can never act silly again, or post your thoughts, or take a stand on an issue about which you feel strongly. But you do need to understand, whether it's fair or not, that anything you post online can affect the views of others and how they evaluate you. You may be the kindest person in the world. You may have graduated with honors. You may even have an exemplary record of community-service involvement. Nevertheless, if you brag online that you were the beer-chugging champ three years in a row, it may be a problem with potential employers. You may also want to reconsider posting photos that show you and your friends half-naked each holding a bottle of vodka.

Exercising restraint and making smart choices regarding your online profile and uploaded content will serve you well in the future. Re-evaluate the benefits of posting personal feelings about someone or taking a controversial stand. You're certainly entitled to your opinions, but so is everyone else. Below are a few thoughts to consider if you choose to have a profile on a social networking website.

- ✔ Companies archive your information that is posted on the Internet. What you post online stays online—forever!
- ✔ Adjusting your privacy setting does *not* guarantee privacy.
- ✔ A simple indiscriminate comment or photo can have lifelong effects.
- ✔ Within a few days of posting your information, it's saved forever.
- ✔ Your information is being archived, even if you've deleted it.
- ✔ If you post enough personal information, your identity can be stolen.
- ✔ Many graduate school admissions offices are now checking profiles.
- ✔ Most corporate recruiters are checking profiles and conducting Internet searches on prospective employees.
- ✔ Be certain that the people who have linked to your site have respectable profiles. You may be guilty by association.
- ✔ College administrators and coaching staffs have been known to visit Facebook to make an assessment about students or monitor their players.
- ✔ Never trust anyone you chat with online. Since you can't see the person's face, you have no way to verify his identity.
- ✔ Never give out your personal information or post any of it online.

✎ Hot Tip:
Don't post anything online that you wouldn't want your mother or boss to see.

I Met Him Online

In an idealistic, "You've Got Mail" world, that would be great. Although it can be tempting to meet people you've been conversing with online, it can also be extremely dangerous! From co-eds who have vanished to *Dateline*'s "To Catch a Predator," it's now evident that some very bad people troll the Internet in search of victims.

The Internet is a predator's dream come true. It's as if it were made just for them. With millions of profiles and chat rooms to select from, predators can stalk their prey in virtual anonymity. Just think about MySpace catching 29,000 registered sex offenders who had profiles. Can you imagine the number of sex offenders and predators they are not aware of?

Many times throughout the school year, the news media will feature a story of a person who's been reported missing. When this occurs, one of the first things the police will do is confiscate the computer to determine the missing person's online habits, including Internet and e-mail history. Sadly, after days and weeks of searching, the person is often found dead.

The entire country has watched in fascination as NBC's Chris Hansen has confronted men who search the Internet for sex from teenagers. What's especially intriguing about *Dateline*'s "To Catch a Predator" is the seeming normalcy of the lives these men lead. They appear to be "everyday guys" who could be living next-door to you right now. Young and old alike, there have been salesmen, firemen, members of the clergy, members of the business community, and government employees caught in the snare of *Dateline*'s net. Their backgrounds are as varied as your neighbors'.

NBC *Dateline* teams up with Perverted Justice, a group who is "on the front lines of the fight against Internet sex predators and the organized pedophilia movement." Their decoys will enter chat rooms as underage kids. If they are solicited for sex by adults, Perverted Justice will "work with police to prosecute and convict those adults." As of August 2007, Perverted Justice has assisted in getting 221 predator convictions.

While Chris Hansen and *Dateline's* "To Catch a Predator" focus on adults who prey on young teenagers, the program should be a constant reminder of the dangerous people who stalk victims on the Internet. The predators featured are not just geographically limited to the programs locale, they are everywhere!

Internet safety and chatting online should still be a top priority while you attend college. It is vitally important that you don't become so overly optimistic that you found "Mr. Right" online that you become naive to the dangers involved. Consider some of these suggestions, precautions, and questions as you're chatting with someone you may have an interest in meeting.

- ✔ How long have you been chatting with this person?
- ✔ Has he shared as much information with you as you have with him?
- ✔ Have you talked on the phone? Have you called him at different times of the day? Does he seem distant or annoyed, or is he rushing you when you call him unexpectedly?
- ✔ Do you know where he works? Have you called him at work? How long has he been employed there?
- ✔ Has he given you his home address, or does he just keep asking for yours?
- ✔ Do you know his cell phone number? Have you called him on it?
- ✔ Do you know what kind of car he drives or what his hobbies are? If you've been chatting for a while online, these should be basic conversational questions.
- ✔ Does he become irritated when you ask a lot of questions of him?
- ✔ If someone you met online is pressuring you to physically meet with him, this should be a red flag to become suspicious of his intentions.

✓ If you do decide to meet with someone you met online, bring a friend along. Never go anywhere with him alone. Also, meet him in a public place and tell your friends where you're going.

✓ Plan with your friend a code word or statement you can use if you would like to leave promptly.

✓ Set ground rules before you meet him. Tell him you would just like to get together for coffee or lunch. Don't meet at a bar and drink alcohol with him.

✓ Limit your time with him on the first few meetings.

✓ If you do decide to meet him, notice his demeanor. Is it similar when you chatted online? Is the car as he described it?

✓ Exercise a great deal of caution and restraint while communicating in chat rooms. You may not even be aware that you are being set-up by a potential predator.

✓ LOOK OUT FOR EACH OTHER!

Cyber Crime

Cyber crime is one of those interesting terms that have multiple meanings. Cyber crime includes using the computer as a tool to actually commit a crime. Conversely, the term "cyber crime" can also refer to somebody becoming a victim of a crime that was perpetrated through the victim's own computer. Cyber crime is a worldwide problem. The U.S. Department of Justice lists the following categories as Internet-related crime.

✓ Computer intrusion (i.e., hacking)
✓ Password trafficking
✓ Counterfeiting of currency
✓ Child pornography or exploitation
✓ Child exploitation and Internet fraud matters that have a mail nexus
✓ Internet fraud and spam
✓ Internet harassment
✓ Internet bomb threats
✓ Trafficking in explosive or incendiary devices or firearms over the Internet

Upskirting

Of all the things in this world that we have to worry about, and it's a lot, we have to add this insane practice to the list. "Upskirting" is a term for when photos are clandestinely taken to view up a woman's skirt. The term "downblousing" may be applied when photos are secretly taken to view down a woman's blouse. Many upskirt and downblousing photos are taken via cell phone cameras. Upskirting has become an entire industry with many websites dedicated to the practice.

The photos can be taken in any location. While walking in your local mall or changing clothes in a dressing room, a hidden camera can be rolling in a variety of creative atmospheres. For example, cameras have been reportedly rigged up in shopping bags with a hole cut out and the lens facing upward. The person carrying the bag will walk very close behind the unsuspecting female while capturing video footage. This video recording could be used for the voyeur's own purposes or possibly uploaded to various Internet websites.

Today, many cameras have lenses that are very small. They can easily be placed in dressing rooms, tanning beds, and inside backpacks. In most states, video voyeurism is illegal in locations where privacy is expected, such as bathrooms and dressing rooms. However, only a few states have passed laws making upskirting or video voyeurism in public illegal.

One successful upskirting technique is when you are shopping and busily looking through the racks of clothes. A person will walk behind you and pretend he has dropped something. As he bends over to pick up the dropped item, he'll take a quick upskirt photo of you. Females must not forget the times in which we live. Cameras are everywhere, and technology is rapidly changing. Since all states don't have laws on the books regarding upskirting and video voyeurism, there is not great deal that can be done should you become a victim. Moreover, if someone posts your photo online, it may be virtually impossible to have the photo removed. With telephoto lenses and innovative voyeurs, females must take extra precautions.

✓ Most importantly, take careful note of your surroundings. Keep a watchful eye on who is around you at all times.

✓ If you are at a party on or off campus, be observant of guests taking pictures.

✓ If you're relaxing in your dormitory, visiting friends on campus, or in any public location, notice who is positioned directly in front of you and behind you.

✓ If you attend sporting events and are sitting in bleachers, be perceptive not only to those near you, but under the bleachers as well.

✓ Be cautious of talking to strangers for any period of time, especially those who may set a package down next to your feet.

✓ Use caution when riding escalators, especially during busy shopping times when there are crowds of people. Consider standing at an angle on the escalator.

✓ If you go to the beach, be very careful of those close to you who may be taking your picture.

Can a Cell Phone Get Me Kicked off the Team?

Quite possibly, yes. It's not the phone per se, as it is the camera in the phone. Do you know of anyone over fifteen who doesn't have a cell phone? If you do, that person is in the minority. A large percentage of Internet postings are taken with cell phone cameras. Many students have digital cameras, but they're not always available when a photo opportunity presents itself.

Cell phones are viewed as being innocuous. They've become so commonplace most people pay no attention to them or to the users. You must be attentive as to who is taking your picture and what they plan on doing with it. Many college parties are packed with students. If you're drinking excessively or partaking in activities that may be questionable, and someone takes your photo and posts it on Facebook, it just may come back to haunt you.

Athletes should take extra caution. College administrators and coaches have high levels of expectations for their athletes. Most schools have campus conduct codes that athletes must follow. Adherence to these conduct codes is strict. If an athlete is in violation of the codes or what could be interpreted as a violation, chances are the athlete will be made an example of what not to do.

An awareness of your surroundings is essential. Whether tailgating, hanging out with friends in your dorm, showering after a game, or watching two people in the midst of an altercation, be conscious of who is taking your picture. Even if photos are taken very innocently, you may have a lot of explaining to do. If you're an athlete, the last thing in the world you need, as well as the university, is bad press. Train yourself to think "camera" when you see a cell phone!

One final note regarding cell phones: should you sign up for a new cell phone package and purchase a new phone, make certain that you delete all your photos and personal information stored in your old phone before you dispose of it.

Cyberstalking

Cyberstalking is when a person uses the Internet or some other electronic means to harass, threaten, or stalk their victim. This can be done through social networking websites, chat rooms, and bulletin boards. It can even be done through text messaging on cell phones.

The organization Working to Halt Online Abuse (WHOA), www.halt abuse.org, "is a volunteer organization founded in 1997 to fight online harassment through education of the general public, education of law enforcement personnel, and empowerment of victims." WHOA's president, Jayne Hitchcock became a victim of cyberstalking in 1996, which in turn led her to become a noted cybercrime and security expert. WHOA receives an estimated fifty to seventy-five cases per week.

The National Center for Victims of Crime (NCVC) offers these suggestions if you believe you're the victim of cyberstalking.

✓ Victims under eighteen should tell their parents or another adult they trust about any harassment and/or threats.

✓ When the offender is known, send the stalker a clear warning. Specifically, communicate that the contact is unwanted and ask the perpetrator to cease sending communications of any kind. Do this only once. Then, no matter the response, under no circumstances should you ever communicate with the stalker again. Save copies of this communication in both electronic and hard copy form.

✓ If the harassment continues, file a complaint with the stalker's Internet service provider, as well as with your own service provider. Many Internet service providers offer tools that filter or block communications from specific individuals.

✓ As soon you suspect you're a victim of online harassment or cyberstalking, start collecting all the evidence and document all contact made by the stalker. Save all e-mail, postings, or other communications in both electronic and hard-copy form. If possible, save all of the header information from e-mails and newsgroup postings. Record the dates and times of any contact with the stalker.

✓ Start a log of each communication explaining the situation in more detail. Document how the harassment is affecting your life and what steps you've taken to stop the harassment.

✓ File a report with local law enforcement or contact their local prosecutor's office to see what charges, if any, can be pursued. Save copies of police reports and record all contact with law enforcement officials and the prosecutor's office.

✓ If you are being continually harassed, consider changing your e-mail address, Internet service provider, or home number, and examine the possibility of using encryption software or privacy protection programs. Any local computer store can offer a variety of protective software, options, and suggestions.

✓ Learn how to use the filtering capabilities of e-mail programs to block e-mails from certain addresses.

✓ Contact online directory listings such as www.four11.com, www.switchboard.com, and www.whowhere.com to request removal from the directory.

✓ Finally, under no circumstances should you agree to meet with the perpetrator face-to-face to "work it out" or "talk." No contact should ever be made with the stalker. Meeting a stalker in person can be very dangerous.

It's Time to Clean Up Your Dirt

I don't mean your dorm room, although goodness knows it could probably use a little dusting. I'm talking cleaning up your computer and the digital dirt that's online about you. "Digital dirt" is a term that refers to any information about you, mostly unflattering information, which is hanging in cyberspace. Profiles on social networking websites like MySpace and Facebook, photos, comments on blogs, and lifestyle choices such as partying and dating can all be considered digital dirt.

Chances are you've already established a profile or have posted comments to blogs and on other people's profiles. Exercise a great deal of restraint with anything you post online, especially in the years before you begin to search for employment. I certainly understand that college life is a time for free expression and just being plain-old silly. However, what you do and say now can have a direct impact on future employment. "Is that fair? No. But it's reality," says David Opton, CEO and founder of ExecuNet, an executive career and business networking organization.

Employers and executive job recruiters are using the Internet as a way to gather information on prospective employees. A 2007 ExecuNet study reports that the number of executive recruiters and hiring managers using Internet search engines to screen and eliminate candidates is growing steadily.

Other groundbreaking research by ExecuNet reveals that digital dirt is helping to shape hiring decisions long before the interview process begins. The following ExecuNet study results show that the influence of online research is on the rise:

	2005	2006	2007
Percentage of recruiters using search engines to learn more about candidates.	75%	77%	83%
Percentage of recruiters that eliminated a candidate based on information found online.	26%	35%	43%

"For better or worse, the Internet provides recruiters and employers with a wealth of unfiltered information that's used to help evaluate candidates," says Dave Opton. "From a candidate's perspective, there's no question that managing your reputation online is as important as it is offline."

A separate survey of 218 executives reveals that while a majority (76 percent) expects companies and recruiters to conduct a search of their name online during the hiring process, 22 percent have never entered their own name into a search engine to determine what personal or professional information is uncovered.

This survey also found that 11 percent of all executives fear that the information found online when entering their name in a search engine could eliminate them from consideration for a new job, and 20 percent have taken proactive steps to increase the positive information found online under their name—up from 13 percent just one year ago.

So what does this all mean to *you*, the college student? It should mean a great deal. The very reason you're going to college is to educate yourself, receive your degree, and hopefully find a position within a company where you can excel and be happy. It would be a travesty for that not to happen because you uploaded photos that showed you drinking while you were half-dressed at an off-campus party.

Photos are but one slice of the pie recruiters may take into account. Be guarded with your choice of words, too. If you decide to boast of your sexual encounters or your loathing of certain groups of people, you may find that you don't receive many requests for interviews. "The trend of recruiters and potential employers researching you online will continue to rise," so says David Opton of ExecuNet.

If you're fortunate enough to secure a position within an organization, it doesn't mean that you can now belittle your manager or disparage the company. Employees have been terminated because of their postings about their employers. Conversely, employees have been dismissed due to postings showing inappropriate conduct outside of the office. It's not just potential employers who are searching the Internet for information in order to make an evaluation about you. Admissions departments in colleges and graduate schools use this practice as well. With limited slots available for graduate school candidates, the Internet is another tool in the prescreening process.

As Internet search technology continues to evolve, recruiters and businesses will fuel the evolution in order to better screen their applicants. The job market is extraordinarily competitive. While it's certainly difficult, and perhaps unrealistic, in a college atmosphere to control everything that's posted online, you must take steps to limit the negative information. Your future employment prospects may depend on it. Take the time to frequently monitor information about you that may be posted on the Internet. Here are some suggestions:

- ✓ Google yourself regularly, especially *before* you begin to search for employment. Find other search engines that will also be able to search for your name.
- ✓ Remove any risqué or uncomplimentary photos.
- ✓ Delete all comments and postings about excessive drinking, doing drugs, or questionable behavior. Even if they're untrue, remove them.
- ✓ Consider removing your profile permanently, especially all unflattering information.
- ✓ Formulate a planned response to prospective employers regarding any negative information that may be exposed.
- ✓ Just because you delete information doesn't mean it's permanently erased. So think about what you want to put online *before* you post it.
- ✓ Think about completely changing your profile.
- ✓ Post positive information about your life and character, such as business endeavors and charitable donations and work, including volunteering for any service-based or community-oriented projects.
- ✓ Obtain your own domain name and post your resume and activities.
- ✓ Don't embellish your qualifications and experience.

I know many of you consider those of us with a little grey hair out of touch when it comes to certain subjects, and technology is no exception. No

one can predict for certain how technology will develop and expand in the future. Rest assured, you will have similar technological challenges with your own children. I can hear you now, "You know, all we had was the Internet. We didn't have these new-fangled devices you kids are using today."

RESOURCES BY CHAPTER

Chapter 1: Life in the Dorms
Center for Campus Fire Safety
P.O. Box 2358
Amherst, MA 01004-2358
www.campusfire.org

Electrical Safety Foundation
International
1300 North 17th Street
Suite 1752
Rosslyn, VA 22209
www.esfi.org

National Fire Sprinkler Association
40 Jon Barrett Road
Patterson, New York 12563
www.nfsa.org

Security on Campus
133 Ivy Lane
Suite 200
King of Prussia, PA 19406-2101
www.securityoncampus.org

Seton Hall University
400 South Orange Avenue
South Orange, NJ 07079
www.shu.edu

State Farm Insurance Company
www.statefarm.com

U.S. Department of Education
www.ed.gov
U.S. Fire Administration
16825 South Seton Avenue
Emmitsburg, MD 21727
www.usfa.dhs.gov

University of South Florida
Counseling Center for Human
Development
East Fowler Avenue
Tampa, FL 33620
www.usfweb2.usf.edu/counsel

Underwriters Laboratories
www.ul.com

Chapter 2: My Safe Campus

Federal Emergency Management Agency
500 C Street SW
Washington, DC 20472
www.fema.gov

International Tactical Officers
Training Org.
P.O. Box 3446
Terre Haute, IN 47803
www.itota.net

National Weather Service
1325 East West Highway
Silver Spring, MD 20910
www.nws.noaa.gov

NOAA
1401 Constitution Avenue, NW
Room 6217
Washington, DC 20230
www.noaa.gov

National Center for Victims of Crime
2000 M Street NW
Suite 480
Washington, DC 20036
www.ncvc.org

Rape, Abuse & Incest National Network
(RAINN)
1-800-656-HOPE (4673)
www.rainn.org

U.S. Department of Justice
www.usdoj.gov

Chapter 3: Would You Like to Go Out Tonight?

Drink Safe Technology
www.drinksafetech.com

National Center for Victims of Crime
2000 M Street NW
Suite 480
Washington, DC 20036
www.ncvc.org

Project GHB, Inc.
www.projectghb.org

Rape, Abuse & Incest National Network
(RAINN)
1-800-656-HOPE (4673)
www.rainn.org

U.S. Department of Health & Human
Services
200 Independence Avenue, SW
Washington, DC 20201
www.os.dhhs.gov

University of South Florida
Counseling Center for Human
Development
East Fowler Avenue
Tampa, FL 33620
www.usfweb2.usf.edu/counsel

Chapter 4: Alcohol and Drugs on Campus

Alcoholics Anonymous
www.alcoholics-anonymous.org

Bowles Center for Alcohol Studies
University of North Carolina at
Chapel Hill
www.med.unc.edu/alcohol

Centers for Disease Control and
Prevention
1600 Clifton Road
Atlanta, GA 30333
www.cdc.gov

National Institute on Alcohol Abuse
and Alcoholism
5635 Fishers Lane MSC 9304
Bethesda, MD 20892-9304
www.niaaa.nih.gov

Pennsylvania Liquor Control Board
www.lcb.state.pa.us

U.S. Department of Education
www.ed.gov

Chapter 5: It's Spring Break!

A Matter of Degree
Harvard School of Public Health
401 Park Drive
Boston, MA 02215
www.hsph.harvard.edu

Alternative Spring Break
2451 Cumberland Parkway
Suite 3124
Atlanta, GA 30339
www.alternativebreaks.org

American Medical Association
515 North State Street
Chicago, IL 60610
www.ama-assn.org

NOAA
1401 Constitution Avenue, NW
Room 6217
Washington, DC 20230
www.noaa.gov

U.S. Department of Justice
www.usdoj.gov

U.S. Lifesaving Association
www.usla.org

University of Wisconsin
www.wisc.edu

Chapter 6: Greek Life and Hazing

Center for Campus Fire Safety
P.O. Box 2358
Amherst, MA 01004-2358
www.campusfire.org

Professor Hank Newer – Author
www.hanknewer.blogspot.com

Matthew Carrington
www.wemissyoumatt.com

Stop Hazing
www.stophazing.org

U.S. Department of Justice
www.usdoj.gov

U.S. Lifesaving Association
www.usla.org

University of Wisconsin
www.wisc.edu

Chapter 7: I Owe More Than My School Loans

Federal Trade Commission – Fair
Credit Bill
600 Pennsylvania Avenue, NW
Washington, DC 20580
www.ftc.gov

Federal Trade Commission – Identity Theft
600 Pennsylvania Avenue, NW
Washington, DC 20580
www.ftc.gov

Nelli Mae
www.nelliemae.com

U.S. Department of Education
www.ed.gov

Chapter 8: *Wheels on Campus*
AAA
www.aaa.com

Federal Bureau of Investigation
www.fbi.gov

Insurance Information Institute
110 William Street
New York, NY 10038
www.iii.org

Mr. Peter J. Johnson, Jr., Esq.
Leahey & Johnson, P.C.
120 Wall Street
New York, NY 10005
www.leaheyandjohnson.com

National Insurance Crime Bureau
www.nicb.org

Chapter 9: *Living Off Campus*
Center for Campus Fire Safety
P.O. Box 2358
Amherst, MA 01004-2358
www.campusfire.org

Insurance Research Council
718 Providence Road
Malvern, PA 19355-0725
www.ircweb.org

State Farm Insurance
www.statefarm.com

Chapter 10: *The World Is Just a Click Away*
Dateline - MSNBC
To Catch a Predator
www.msnbc.msm.com

ExecuNet
295 Westport Avenue
Norwalk, CT 06851
www.execunet.com

Facebook
www.facebook.com

MySpace
www.myspace.com

National Center for Victims of Crime
2000 M Street, NW
Suite 480
Washington, DC 20036
www.ncvc.org

Perverted Justice
www.perverted-justice.com

U.S. Department of Justice
www.usdoj.gov

Working to Halt Online Abuse – WHOO
P.O. Box 782
York, ME 03909
www.haltabuse.org

ABOUT THE AUTHOR

Thomas M. Kane is President of the College Safety Zone, an advocacy and consulting group on campus security and safety issues. He speaks to college administrators, public safety officials, and high school and college students. He is a member of the Association for the Promotion of Campus Activities. He is the author of _Priests Are People, Too!_ (Thomas More Publishing, 2002). He has appeared on _ABC News_ in Pittsburgh, _The O'Reilly Factor, CNN's Crossfire, The God Squad_, MSNBC with Alan Keyes; _FOX Wire_ with Rita Cosby, _At Large with Geraldo Rivera_, and appeared with _FOX News_ anchor John Gibson. Mr. Kane has been featured on hundreds of talk-radio programs throughout the United States and Canada. He has also been featured in newspapers from Alaska to Florida.

The College Safety Zone's website is www.collegesafetyzone.com.